1991

REVIEWING THE ARTS

COMMUNICATION TEXTBOOK SERIES
Jennings Bryant—Editor

Journalism
Maxwell McCombs—Advisor

BERNER • Writing Literary
Features

FENSCH • The Sports Writing
Handbook

TITCHENER • Reviewing
the Arts

REVIEWING THE ARTS

Campbell B. Titchener
University of Houston

LEA LAWRENCE ERLBAUM ASSOCIATES, PUBLISHERS
1988 Hillsdale, New Jersey   Hove and London

Lawrence Erlbaum Associates, Inc., Publishers
365 Broadway
Hillsdale, New Jersey 07642

Cover, production and interior
 design: Robin Marks Weisberg

Library of Congress Cataloging-in-Publication Data

Titchener, Campbell B.
   Reviewing the arts / Campbell B. Titchener.
       p.   cm.
   "Houston, Texas, 1987."
   ISBN 0-8058-0237-1
   1. Newspapers—Columns, sections, etc.—Reviews. 2. Newspapers—Columns, sections, etc.—
Arts. 3. Art criticism. 4. Journalism—Authorship. 5. American newspapers—Columns, sec-
tions, etc.—Reviews. 6. American newspapers—Columns, sections, etc.—Arts. 7. Art criticism—
United States. 8. Journalism—United States—Authoriship. I. Title
PN4784.R4T58 1988
070.4'497—dc19

                                                                              88-453
                                                                              CIP

Printed in the United States of America
10 9 8 7 6 5 4 3 2 1

Contents

v

Preface

This book is written for those generalists in the media who find themselves faced with the prospect of reviewing an artistic event or performance, and for those who teach and train journalism students.

Nowhere, it seems, are there rules or guidelines to follow, and precious few helpful hints.

On small daily and weekly newspapers in particular, the budding journalist with a feeling for the arts often is told "just look in the files for examples from the guy before you." It gives one pause. Such advice serves only to perpetuate mediocrity.

Reviewing the Arts is designed to help the writer produce an acceptable review, and also deals with other tasks normally handled by the amusements or entertainment staff.

This work suggests ways to approach familiar, and unfamiliar, art forms in order to prepare an informed evaluation. It is supported by examples from ordinary journalists and veteran critics. All contributors have shared the trepidation of being assigned to cover an unfamiliar event. They represent different geographical areas of the country, and vary widely in age and number of years on the job.

The examples presented are not necessarily illustrative of the best of this type of writing, but are representative of the many excellent reviews written against a deadline that appear in the nation's press.

Some of these writers have moved on, but in this book they are associated with the publications for which they worked when they contributed not only the examples found here, but also experiences and ideas about the newspaper and entertainment business as well.

The question of nomenclature must be addressed. We speak of critics, reviewers, entertainment writers, feature writers, arts writers, lifestyle writers, and more.

But the distinction that must be made is between the two types of opinionated writing about the arts—the review and the criticism—which is discussed in chapter 1.

This book does not deal specifically with television and radio broadcasts, because commentary in those media is, of necessity, limited to a few paragraphs at best. In addition, the highly rated critics who appear weekly on TV have the tremendous advantage of being able to show clips from films. And, an important distinction, they view the films they criticize alone. They are obviously unable to include audience reaction in their analyses.

However, the approach one would take in those media to evaluating an art would be basically the same as is presented here. Chapter 3 is written for the print journalist, but can serve the broadcaster as well.

The author describes the activities of a mythical critic (she) and a mythical reviewer (he). The hope is that this he-she, his-her usage makes a natural distinction for the comparison of the two types of writing, reviews and criticisms.

The principles presented here are a result of the author's 30 years experience as entertainment writer and teacher, and reflect the methods employed by most contemporary writers.

ACKNOWLEDGMENTS

Those who contributed examples and anecdotes about the reviewing business deserve the author's heartfelt thanks, as do their publishers who have generously given their permission to reprint these examples. They include Kay Gardella, The New York *Daily News*; Dennis Hunt, the Los Angeles *Times*; Anthony Bannon and Jack Foran, the Buffalo *Evening News*; Dee Ann Rexroat and Les Zachels of the Cedar Rapids *Gazette*; Kathryn Bernheimer and Jane Fudge, the Boulder *Daily Camera*; Tom Carter, of the Lexington *Herald-Leader*; Steve Morse, The Boston *Globe*; Janna Q. Anderson, Fargo *Forum*; Edward J. Osowski of Houston; Don Houser of Highland, Indiana; and John Hurst, Alfred Key, Robert Masullo, and particularly William Glackin, of the Sacramento *Bee*. And all of us are forever in debt to Brooks Atkinson.

Old friends Ann Holmes of the Houston *Chronicle* and Eric Gerber of the Houston *Post* provided not only helpful material, but also encouragement and enthusiasm. Invariably, we did not agree on all aspects of the wonderful world of reviewing the arts, but we were philosophically very close; what appears in these pages is a consensus.

But these writers who have provided their writing and their advice are only one of three groups who deserve credit for the conception and preparation of the book. Thanks also go to those who have appeared on stage, on various screens, in print and on exhibit during the past half century—those who, as Hollywood would say, produced the product. All played a part in this, as did those who reported on their activities.

Thanks go, also, to the members of the various arts faculties at the University of Houston who offered suggestions for further reading.

Finally, the students. In 1964 I walked into a classroom at The Ohio State University to teach a class in the writing of reviews and criticisms, and I have been at it at one place or another ever since. Those students, and others who have sat in similar classrooms in almost a quarter of a century since, were indispensable. Their writing, their ideas, their questions and comments, and some of their work, is in these pages.

Chapter One
The Critic and the Reviewer

The two enter the theater through different doors. Taking seats near the end of the aisle on the third row they nod briefly in recognition. It is not quite 5 minutes before the curtain is to go up. Each opens a program and studies it intently.

Behind them, a patron whispers to a companion: "They're the critics."

She works for a large daily newspaper and is present this evening to offer her comments on a new play about to be acted by a local professional group. His job is with a smaller newspaper, one with circulation primarily in the suburbs. She is a critic, he is a reviewer. Each will write about the evening's offering for the next day's newspaper.

These two writers seem to be engaged in similar occupations. To the reading public at home a critic is a critic is a critic. Inside the professional newsroom, however, the difference becomes apparent and important. To begin this discussion of covering the arts for newspapers of all sizes, it helps to take a closer look at these two, and the hundreds of writers they represent, and to define their activities, responsibilities, and areas of interest and expertise.

They perform similar functions, but in different roles, which is why to the reader they seem to be identical. A closer look shows that, to a large degree, the similarities are only surface. Briefly, she is an experienced critic, specializing in only one art form and, for the most part, confining her activities to reviewing new openings, and offering occasional provocative, longer essays on the arts. This writing is properly called *criticism*. It is most often found on the front page of the entertainment section of the Sunday edition of her newspaper.

He is a member of an entertainment staff, and performs a variety of functions, one of which is reviewing new plays. He might glance wistfully at his neighbor and think "How nice to be able to concentrate on one art." Still, he does enjoy the variety his job offers, and there is too much to do to spend time thinking about the other side of the street.

THE CRITICISM AND THE REVIEW

Composer-critic Lehman Engel put it best in his book *The Critics*[1] when he explained the difference between a studied evaluation over time of an artistic effort (criticism), and the overnight reaction to a play, concert, or exhibit (review). To sharpen the distinction, the criticism normally appears days, even weeks, after the event in question. It reflects the critic's studied thought; she must be given ample time to decide on the ultimate value of what she has seen. Although her review will be in tomorrow's newspaper, the timing of her criticism is of relatively little importance. As she watches this new play unfold, she is thinking not only of the review, but also of a possible criticism she will write for later publication, perhaps comparing this new effort with other works, by the same playwright as well as others.

The review, however, must appear as soon as possible after the opening. No one wants to read (or for that matter write) a review that will not appear until well after its object has opened. Her associate will dash back to the office, put together his review, and then, more than likely, turn to other entertainment desk activities. His interest in this new play will soon diminish.

Now it is the next day, and the critic clips her review for filing, and makes some notes on her reactions that did not make it into print. As with other reviewers, she was pressed for time and was able to present only a surface analysis of this play. She will spend a fair amount of time in the days to come rethinking her position, reading from a collection of reference books, perhaps even returning to the theater to see it again. Then she will write a criticism. She spends almost all her time with plays, playwrights, directors, and producers.

Most critics are experts in their fields, and when a play or musical composition or film has general acceptance as a work of enduring quality, it is usually the collective opinion of the critics that places it in that lofty category. Therefore, it is the critic's primary role to assign what she sees to a place in history. Reviewing that effort for the next day's paper is a smaller aspect of her occupation.

Across town he also clips his review, turns to a file cabinet, reaches past the drawers marked "Art" and "Music" to "Theater," opens the drawer and slides the clip into a folder marked "New"—and the current year. He may or may not ever have occasion to look it up, but if need be he can find it in an instant.

Duties on the Entertainment Desk

Now he spends some time laying out pages for the next day's entertainment section;

---

[1]Engel, L. (1976). *The critics*. New York: Macmillan.

perhaps checks on the accuracy of TV listings carried over from the previous week; sorts through a large stack of mail from film and television producers, networks, public relations firms with glamorous clients; and a stack of telephone messages. He checks his watch. He is going to see a new Australian film in the afternoon, and the next night he will attend a rock concert in an outdoor theater.

Writers like these are *generalists*, and often are referred to as entertainment writers, considering the variety of their assignments. This one, like most, would like to try his hand at serious criticism, something he can afford to do only rarely. But there is too much going on, too many other responsibilities. If the critic is like the harpist in the orchestra, waiting patiently for her turn to perform her specialty, the entertainment writer is like the percussionist, racing from timpani to bells to xylophone to triangle to snare drum.

Newspapers not able to afford the luxury of a collection of critics nevertheless regularly publish reviews of artistic and creative efforts, but they are produced by entertainment writers. During this discussion it is easier to call them reviewers because when they are functioning in the area of our interest, they are writing reviews. Such criticism as does appear is as likely to be the work of a syndicated or wire service writer. Because many large newspapers with highly regarded critics (*New York Times*, *Los Angeles Times*, *Washington Post*) make their writers' output available through syndication, newspapers without established critics have access to criticism of the highest caliber. Reviews, however, are primarily a local matter.

Both the review and the criticism are subjective pieces of writing. Each deals with the presence or absence of artistic ability and creativity, and each is the product of a writer interested in and concerned about the arts. The differences are in the scope of the writer's activity. The critic normally limits her comments to new, major professional activities, whereas the reviewer gets a shot at anything that comes down the pike. Each develops standards about what deserves attention and what does not, a much easier assignment for the critic. She will write about a group of professional musicians playing a Mozart symphony, as does he, but he also draws the Jamaican rhythm band playing on sawed-off oil drums. Then comes the fellow who blows across the tops of partially filled bottles to produce a series of tones. She will have none of this; he can only hope he does not have to.

They Begin in Different Ways

Those who review for a living often begin their careers on small newspapers, developing a familiarity with the arts as well as an acceptable writing style and, of considerable importance, a knowledge of the newspaper business.

Critics may have taken this path, or may have come from the arts. An ongoing argument rages over whether it is easier to teach an artist journalism, or a journalist an art. Reviewers normally have followed the latter trail; critics, as often as not, the former.

The critics who write for the *New York Times* represent years of close, professional association with the arts, yet there are other highly regarded newspapers that boast of legitimate critics. The Charlotte, North Carolina, *Observer*, a fairly large (circulation 190,000 daily, 255,000 Sunday) newspaper but still less than one-fifth the size of the *New York Times*, at one time had a critical staff with credentials that would do justice to its prestigious neighbor. The theater critic was educated in theater, the music and dance critic was a trained musician and dancer, and the popular music critic was also a performer. In addition, the book editor was a published author. This newspaper correctly considers its arts writers to be critics, and is convinced that critics should have experience as performers.

This view is shared to a degree by noted playwright Edward Albee,[2] who told a class of student journalists that he felt all critics should have been performers or artists. He said, however, that he himself would like to be an art or sculpture critic, fields he said he knows something about, rather than a drama critic as a student had suggested. Albee's reasoning was that familiarity with the creative process and knowledge of a medium should allow a critic to move from field to field.

On the other hand, there are certainly many reviewers who have never performed, yet have developed considerable expertise in their field.

The View from Sacramento

Such is the situation at the Sacramento, California, *Bee*, where the circulation is actually slightly higher than in Charlotte (228,000 daily, 264,000 Sunday). There a group of generalists, all able to work with various members of the creative and artistic community, handles critical activities for the greater Sacramento area as well as major events in San Francisco. William Glackin, who has been reviewing for *The Bee* for more than a quarter of a century, agreed that most reviews are done by entertainment generalists rather than critics.[3] He offered this definition:

> The distinction between critics and reviewers is an arbitrary one and, in a sense, artificial, but it has its uses in understanding what newspaper reviewing should be. It is a question of emphasis. The determining factors include the audience, space, time, and equipment of the writer. One might say simply that a critic is a man who has a lot of time to think about his views, plenty of space to write about them, readers who already know the background of what he is talking about, and the authoritative knowledge (and, let us hope, sagacity) to locate a given work of art in a meaningful place in the whole history of art. A reviewer, on the other hand, is a fellow who tries to tell you, pretty much in terms of personal description, what happened with the art and what the experience was like.

---

[2]Edward Albee's remarks were made as a guest speaker at a journalism class at the University of Houston in the Spring of 1986.

[3]The following are excerpts from a three-part series, "Reviewing the Arts for a Newspaper" that appeared in The Sacramento *Bee*, May–June, 1967.

Glackin (1967) continued:

When people start talking about newspaper reviewing, sooner or later the talk gets around to the qualifications a reviewer should have. Inevitably, somebody will insist he ought to be as expert as the artist himself. "If you're not a musician, what gives you the right to tell them how to play?" Aside from the fact that the reviewer ought to be writing more about what they are playing than how, the remark is twice confused. It regards the reviewer primarily as a judge, rather than a reporter, reversing what should be the order of emphasis. (This is a confusion often compounded, unfortunately, by reviewers themselves.) And it confuses the act of making art with the act of perceiving it. Or, as somebody once said, "You don't have to lay an egg to know when one is rotten."

Newspapers of all sizes are concerned with the arts, and the circulation of the paper is not necessarily an indication of the way the arts are treated. The attitude of the community is an important factor as, of course, is the attitude of the publisher.

Attitude Counts as Much as Size

It would be wrong to assume that a comparatively small newspaper would pay little or no attention to covering events of artistic interest. *The Daily Camera* in Boulder, Colorado, with a circulation around 30,000, likes to boast that "it doesn't know it's little," and also boasts of an entertainment staff of four full-time and two part-time people. The full timers function as entertainment writers, handling all the routine assignments of the entertainment desk.

At one time the *Camera* had a film and theater critic with a master's degree in theater, a music critic with an undergraduate degree in English who played five musical instruments, and a TV writer with a degree in communications and English. A generalist on the staff had a degree in art history. But, as Features Editor Patty Burnett explained, the degrees were not the reasons these people were hired. They were chosen primarily because they could write.

Things were not quite the same at the Fargo, North Dakota, *Forum*, with a circulation twice that of the Boulder newspaper. That paper gets by with one entertainment writer, and before Janna Anderson arrived on the scene, entertainment news was handled by a police reporter.

Tom Lounges was too busy studying the arts to graduate from college, thus can claim neither performance nor academic credentials. Nevertheless he became an entertainment writer for the Gary, Indiana, *Post-Tribune* and the Hammond, Indiana, *Times*, in addition to editing his own publication, an entertainment tabloid called *The Illiana Beat*. He still gives occasional guest lectures at colleges and universities on interviewing and the arts.

The interested artist or journalist can find no clear path to follow to secure a position as either entertainment writer or critic. Clearly a strong interest in the arts and an ability to use the language are the requisites. Next comes an understanding of the newspaper business, whether it is gleaned from journalism classes, an internship, or learned on the job.

Editors of smaller newspapers often look to their general assignment reporters when they want to add to the amusements or entertainment staff. There may well be a former piano student, amateur actor, or budding artist in the newsroom. That person, at least, knows the newspaper business generally, and is probably the first choice for a new face on the arts and entertainment desk. An existing employee does not have to be taught reporting and interviewing, and probably has some idea of laying out pages, editing copy, and writing headlines, all typical entertainment desk activities.

THE ADVANCE

A common subject for anybody on the entertainment, features, or amusements desk is the advance. An advance story is an announcement of, or feature on, a coming attraction, and advance stories take up a sizable part of the entertainment pages. In particular, small dailies without the manpower or news services to fill their pages with current events rely heavily on these stories.

Some coming attractions, such as the annual visit of a major ice show, may require as many as 6 advances. Others, more routine, will get one. The advances can be written by the promoters bringing the attractions to town, a local public relations firm, or by the local newspaper staff. In the event of a major event such as a circus, there is usually an advance man who arrives in town at least 2 weeks ahead of opening day. His job is to provide the local media with photos, story lines, biographies of stars, and to arrange interview opportunities once the show itself arrives.

His material is professionally done, and can be used almost as is. Of course it does lean a little heavily on the excitement and splendor, and is not really the objective writing the editor prefers. But it provides the information the entertainment writer needs for his own advance, and is valuable.

Another source for the advance is a local public relations firm that has contracted with the producers of a touring production to handle advance copy. The rules here are the same. It is good copy, but needs editing.

Here are the first two paragraphs of a typical release mailed to a newspaper in advance of an attraction:

> "Sugar Babies," Broadway's smash burlesque musical starring Mickey Rooney and Ann Miller opens a three week engagement at the Music Hall, Tuesday, April 26 through Sunday, May 15. The show is presented by Houston Grand Opera Productions, Inc., and Pace Theatrical Group, Inc., as part of their Broadway Star premiere season.
>
> Described as the "ultimate burlesque musical," "Sugar Babies" is a million dollar burlesque show replete with fourteen show girls, a male ensemble, a gallery of comics, fan dancers, a tribute to Little Egypt, a candy butcher, a juggling comedian with a

fetish for bowling balls, a strip tease, an opera interlude, a minstrel number, blackouts and sketches, a ventriloquist, a soubrette covered in live doves, a rousing patriotic finale and dozens of other treats, including two of the greatest stars ever seen on the musical stage, the legendary Mickey Rooney and Ann Miller.

The release could have appeared just as it was received; certainly the company handling local arrangements had skilled writers familiar with the newspaper's readers. Yet most editors would balk at running this as is. Basic style errors would have to be corrected, but the main fault is that the sponsors appear unnecessarily high in the copy. A simple rewrite would turn this into an acceptable advance story:

> "Sugar Babies," the Broadway musical starring Mickey Rooney and Ann Miller, will open a three-week engagement at the Music Hall Tuesday, April 26. The show will run through May 15.
>
> The musical is based on old-time vaudeville and burlesque shows, and features show girls, comics, dancers, jugglers, a strip tease, an opera interlude, a ventriloquist, a patriotic finale, and a candy butcher, the theatrical term for a person who moves through the audience during the program selling candy.

The adjectives need not be part of the advance, and if the entertainment writer wants to keep language such as "candy butcher" or "soubrette" he should be prepared to define his terms.

Good Advance Copy Is Welcome

There is nothing sacred about the copy that the advance man sends, nor is there any copyright protection. The local writer can do as he wishes with the material. Of course he would not change the facts or the content, but he will feel free to alter the form. From the advance man's standpoint, the best thing that could happen is that his release appears untouched. But that is not very likely, so the next best thing is that part of it, or the gist of it, gets published. The worst of all worlds is when nothing shows up in the paper. So he is grateful for all favors, and is available to give help as needed.

Larger newspapers often develop their own advance material, sometimes by calling the promoters with specific questions, and sometimes by sending a writer to the city where the attraction is currently playing. Locally generated copy is always best, editors agree, but the cost of producing it can be formidable. The typical entertainment writer learns to work with what he is sent, and becomes proficient at weeding out the puffery.

Amateurs Need Help

Professionally produced advance copy saves the local staff time and money, and makes the job of filling the entertainment pages easier. But good advance material is not always available, particularly when the attraction in question is locally produced. When amateurs are in charge of publicity, the well sometimes runs dry.

Well-intentioned publicity chairpersons elected by their peers are not always familiar with newspaper practices, particularly when it comes to deadlines. They will submit copy far too early or way too late, then wonder why the newspaper was not interested in what they had to offer. In some cases, an amateur publicist will mistakenly assume that the newspaper routinely keeps track of all coming events, and just as routinely sends reporters and photographers to cover them. Or it might be that a similar activity the previous year was covered in the paper, and the group assumes that it will be again.

Few things are as painful for the entertainment editor as the telephone call late in the afternoon, with a person on the other end saying "You know, our play opens tonight. You will send someone out, won't you?" And this need not happen. The first step is for the entertainment desk to supply all local artists with lists of deadlines, photo requirements, addresses where to send material, and telephone numbers where questions can be answered. The second step is to hope these suggestions are followed.

Enter the Profit Motive

Experienced entertainment editors know that when money is charged for tickets and someone stands to make a profit, there will be no shortage of advance material. To the pros, publicity means ticket sales and ticket sales mean money in their pockets. And even though there is a charge to attend the amateur production, most proceeds go for props, play rental, and to build up enough of a war chest to some day hire a real director (or conductor or choreographer). When local amateurs are in charge of publicity, they will need help.

THE TELEVISION PREVIEW

An increasingly popular form of advance story is the television preview, a combination of advance and review. Syndicates and wire services are good sources for these, which need little or no editing, because the writers are employed by news agencies, not promoters, and therefore have no stake in the success of the venture. This is a syndicated *New York Daily News* preview by Kay Gardella (1984)[4] of a prime-time television attraction:

---

[4]Copyright, 1984, New York News Inc. Reprinted with permission.

ROBIN HOOD WAS NEVER THIS ZANY

By Kay Gardella
New York Daily News

George Segal, star of A Touch of Class, Who's Afraid of Virginia Woolf? and the TV film Trackdown: Finding the Goodbar Killer, may be an unlikely choice to play Robin Hood. But in The Zany Adventures of Robin Hood (8:30 tonight, CBS), he stars in a wild-and-woolly parody on the Sherwood Forest hero who stole from the rich to give to the poor.

Made on location at an English castle, the film stacks up as good family fun, as 12th-century England gets a fast paint job with 20th-century humor. Co-starring are Morgan Fairchild as the fair Maid Marian and Roddy McDowell as the scheming Prince John, who stands to profit if his brother, Richard the Lionhearted (Robert Hardy), is not returned to the throne. Richard has been captured during the Crusades and is held hostage by Duke Leopold of Austria. His mother, Eleanor of Aquitaine, is played by Janet Suzman.

As the spoof opens, Prince John is seeing his psychiatrist. "How can I be loved as a prince if I were never loved as a child?" he sighs. The shrink, whose parents are in the castle dungeons as prisoners of the prince, is forced to tell John only what he wants to hear.

"If torturing people and pillaging villages makes you feel good, then do it," the doctor advises.

It's Prince John's birthday feast, and the entire court in attendance sings "For he's a jolly good fellow, which nobody'd better deny." He seems bored with the proceedings until someone disguised as a woman arrives to sing him a vicious telegram, supposedly from Robin Hood, a devoted follower of King Richard, who lived in Sherwood Forest. As it turns out, the "woman" is the outlaw himself.

Maid Marian has a problem, too. In order to keep her promise to King Richard to remain a virgin, she takes cold dips in the castle moat. One thing, and one thing only, is on her mind, and she makes her desire clear to Eleanor, who has decided the two should enter Sherwood Forest to raise the ransom money for King Richard.

Dressed as nuns, they journey into the forest as the plot and jokes thicken and Marian falls for Robin Hood. "Is it Robyn or Robin?" she asks.

Also typical of the humor you'll encounter is this: When Robin Hood stops a coach, the driver calls it a "no-frills peasant run." Mel Brooks had nothing to do with this film, but it's definitely his style of comedy.

The TV preview is usually long on summary, and normally contains opinion, or at least a suggestion of the program's probable success. But this opinion is expressed in a review, as in this example, rather than a criticism.

THE CELEBRITY INTERVIEW

An eye-catching feature on any page is an interview with a celebrity, particularly in the entertainment section, where the names of the stars are household words. Interviews are personality sketches, and usually include some elements of the advance and the review. An interview with a television series star is interesting; if that star is coming to your town soon, the interview is very interesting. If the interview is accompanied by a candid photo taken by your staff, even better.

Actors, artists, and authors give interviews because they are expected to and accept the assignment as part of their occupation; because they genuinely want to, and are pleased with the publicity; or because it is part of their contracts. The actor in a traveling show gets paid regardless of the size of the audience, whereas the promoter makes money only if the crowds are substantial. It is not surprising, then, that promoters often insist that their stars make themselves available for interviews.

It Is a Job for the Entertainment Writer

The successful interview is part news story, part feature, and is entertaining. The reader should learn something new and be interested in, or amused by, the article. The writer's task is to be prepared, to know what kind of questions the readers will hope to see answered, and how to elicit good quotes from the subject. And this requires homework. Every entertainment writer knows that looking up the star's record (and every entertainment desk is bombarded with publicity material from all sides) is the first step. The interview should be a pleasant social event, a discussion between writer and subject. Each should be pleased with the result, so it is normally a cooperative venture. When the subject is hostile, or less than friendly, the interviewer should remember his newsroom training, particularly the part about how to handle the unfriendly subject.

JoAnn Rhetts (personal communication, January, 1984) in Charlotte, North Carolina, a serious and conscientious interviewer, had to laugh when a subject told her he thought a good interview should be, for both interviewer and interviewee, like a fruitful session of psychotherapy.

Tom Carter (personal communication, January, 1984) in Lexington, Kentucky, is one who believes in taping a telephone interview, with the subject's permission, of course, but that is not always possible. When he met with jazz pianist Oscar Peterson he had to settle for a brief talk in the hallway of a high-rise hotel in Atlanta. But he had prepared well, and those brief moments provided enough questions and answers to flesh out an interesting and well-received interview.

Carter had discovered, as all professionals eventually do, that the public response to an article or interview has nothing to do with the time invested in producing it. In this instance a lot of time went into the preparation, the homework, and only a small amount was spent on the actual interview.

Janna Anderson (personal communication, December, 1983), when in comparatively remote Fargo, spent a lot of time on the telephone. She included as part of her normal homework reading *American Film*, *Rolling Stone*, and *TV Guide*, as well as keeping a regular eye on "Entertainment Tonight" on television. When the telephone rang, she had plenty to talk about.

William Glackin (personal communication, January, 1984) in Sacramento admitted to a jaundiced view of the telephone interview. He feels it is rare to find a subject who tells you anything worth knowing. "Rather than phone somebody in San Francisco, we commonly send somebody down to do the job in person," he said. "We have nine cars in the editorial department, which reduces expenses for the paper." Nice, if the budget allows.

In the final analysis, entertainment interviewing is reporting. This syndicated feature by Hunt[5] illustrates the interviewer at his best. Not surprisingly, it got wide play in American newspapers.

TINY TIM KNOCKS; WILL OPPORTUNITY REOPEN?

By Dennis Hunt
Los Angeles Times Syndicate

Tiny Tim blew it.

In the late '60s, the eccentric pop singer became a national sensation singing off-beat songs like Tiptoe Through the Tulips in that quivery high-pitched voice, accompanying himself on ukelele. Everyone was laughing at the big, middle-aged man who behaved like a shy schoolgirl.

He appeared frequently on TV shows such as Johnny Carson's Tonight Show as well as Rowan and Martin's Laugh-In. His 1969 marriage to 17-year-old Miss Vicki on the Carson show was a national event. (The marriage, which ended in 1974, produced a daughter who now lives with her mother.)

Many think that Tiny Tim is living comfortably in retirement on the money he made in his heyday. Instead, he is living frugally in a modest New York hotel with his 90-year-old mother. He is struggling—working bars and obscure clubs and guest-starring in an occasional rock'n'roll show.

What happened?

One recent morning, while he was in Ontario, Calif., to perform in a rock show at a high school in this town about 40 miles east of Los Angeles, he tried to explain it.

His room was sweltering. He complained that the air conditioning was malfunctioning. It turned out that he had accidentally turned on the heat instead. "It may be my fault," he acknowledged sheepishly. "I do silly things sometimes."

Tiny Tim was never really tiny; he is 6-foot-1. Even in his heyday he was pudgy, and since then he has gained quite a few pounds, mostly around the waist.

But basically, even at 55, he is the same old Tiny Tim—the lovable, coquettish kook with the beakish nose, disheveled, stringy hair and white makeup. He was wearing a blue tuxedo jacket with wildly clashing purple shirt and green polka-dot tie. His jogging shoes didn't seem out of place at all.

When Tiny Tim talks, people listen. That morning, he was speaking with evangelical fervor, waving his arms in melodramatic flourishes, rolling his eyes toward the ceiling to highlight important points.

Discussing his career decline really got him worked up. "I was on top for a while," he boasted. "It was great. I was a big star. Then all of a sudden it was gone; I was back at the bottom. It was horrible. I didn't know what hit me. I should have had a lot of money but I didn't."

His business associates, he charged, were at fault for mismanaging his earnings. "I never saw any of the money I made," he insisted. "They used to give me $100 a week; if I needed something extra, I could call someone and get it. But I never saw any of my big money."

It was not surprising that Tiny Tim wasn't hot very long. Traditionally, novelty acts are like shooting stars. By the early '70s, he had flamed out.

Born Herbert Buckingham Khaury in New York, Tiny Tim started out as a standard crooner, initially copying Bing Crosby. But his singing career, begun in the '40s, went nowhere. In the early '50s he decided it was time for a change.

"I saw the problem," he said. "I wasn't original; I sounded like everyone else. It was time to be different."

His prayers, he insisted, were the key. "I'm very religious. I prayed and prayed and I found the way. One morning I woke up and I felt like this high voice was in me. So I started singing that way. It was very original."

To enhance his originality, he let his hair grow and started wearing white makeup. "The makeup gave me a feeling of purity," he explained. "People thought I was weird; people in New York used to make fun of me and take pictures of me. My relatives turned away from me; my parents didn't understand. But I found solace in the Lord."

In 1960 his manager named him Sir Timothy Thames, one of a long line of colorful stage names. It did not catch on, so the manager modified it to Tiny Tim.

He worked as a messenger to supplement his income from clubs while waiting for a break, which finally came in 1967 when a Warner Bros. executive signed him. In his heyday, Tiny Tim recorded three albums for Warner Bros. Since then, he has not recorded another in the United States.

More than anything else, Tiny Tim wants to be a big star again. "I know I can do it one more time," he said, the fervor rising in his voice. "I remember how great it was—I was meeting all the stars, I was in demand, I was going everywhere. The feeling of being on top is a great feeling, an incomparable feeling."

There is another reason for his determination to recapture stardom. "I am in love with this lovely woman, Miss Jan," he explained. "Her parents say I'm a has-been. I want to prove they're wrong."

At his age, the odds are staggeringly against him resurrecting his career, but he refuses to acknowledge that. "I'm going to keep trying and trying until I make it big again," he said, pounding the table after each "trying."

In 1982 he recorded two unsuccessful albums in Australia. Since his days at Warner Bros. in the late '60s, his only American records, such as the 1980 single Yummy, Yummy Pizza have been flops for small American labels.

His latest single, I'm Just a Lonesome Clone, written by New York singer-songwriter Lou Stevens, is due to be released soon on Stevens' Clone Records.

And not too long ago he recorded two songs in Australia that he feels are potential hits. One is a song by the heavy-metal band ACDC, Highway to Hell; the other is the old Rod Stewart hit, Do Ya Think I'm Sexy?

What he really wants is a contract with an American label. Meanwhile, he is working on keeping his act current, mixing oldies like Baby Face and Heartbreak Hotel with current hits.

"My show is up to the minute," he said. "I can sing what the young people want to hear. Let me sing Beat It (the Michael Jackson hit) for you."

He sang a few lines, sounding like a parody of an old-fashioned crooner. It was hilarious. So were his abbreviated versions of Marvin Gaye's Sexual Healing and Rick James' Super Freak.

Then he started talking about making it to the top again, repeating most of what he had already said. Once more, with great enthusiasm, he vowed: "I'm going to try and try and try until it finally happens." Again, he pounded the table three times, one for each "try."

Keeping the Office Up to Date

In addition to preparing material for the entertainment pages, the staff is obliged to do a certain amount of record keeping. Reviewers, critics, and columnists often find themselves referring to the recent or distant past. It helps to have copies of reviews close at hand, as well as lists of best-selling books, Top Ten record charts, top-grossing films, award winners in all the arts, and current fact books. The entertainment staff may receive as many calls for information as the sports desk, and should be prepared.

What is needed next is a close examination of the art of the review—what is reviewed, and how to do it.

Chapter Two
The Seven Lively Arts— And More!

A reviewer charged with covering the arts might deal with all of them, eventually, but in only a few years, he will become familiar with at least four or five.

He will not find moving from one to the other difficult if he considers each from a basic perspective as a performing (active) or a fine (passive) art. Then, by recognizing and evaluating the element of creativity, he will be able to apply a basic formula (chap. 3) to any of them to produce a review.

Seven of the arts, architecture, art, dance, drama, literature, music, and sculpture, are considered traditional. Radio–television and film are called *modern*, or *plastic*, arts.

Some would add photography to that list, and with good cause. The work of skilled photographers such as the late Ansel Adams, Edward Steichen, and Alfred Stieglitz, is exhibited and sold in galleries, along with more traditional depictments.

An argument could also be made for computer art, no longer a rarity, and graphic arts in general. The graphic artist can be creative and his product appealing, but the question ''Is it art?'' has yet to be answered. The safest path for now is to consider all these various applications as art, rather than attempt to develop new and distinct categories.

Sculpture is another form of expression not clearly defined. It is a traditional art when an artist has formed some kind of three-dimensional object of more-or-less permanent material. But what of sculpture made of found objects? Is a piece of driftwood shaped by the seas and attached to a plastic base art? If it looks like art, is it automatically art? If it gives satisfaction to the beholder, is it not art?

Originality Versus Creativity

Fortunately, it is not necessary to make a distinction between creativity and originality, between genius and imitation, between mortal and divine intervention (as with the driftwood). If the object on display represents originality, craft, or talent, and reflects some degree of creativity, it can be reviewed.

Some art forms obviously attract more notice than others. Architecture would seem to excite the least attention, unless the event is truly spectacular. Sculpture does not rank high among the popular arts in terms of audience and newspaper coverage, although the increased interest on many university campuses in commissioned sculpture, as well as the interest on the part of developers to enhance a downtown building site with a new creation, is growing.

Dance, as a subject, often seems to depend on the location of the newspaper. If there is an active dance community, perhaps a magnet high school specializing in the arts, there may be a modest amount of activity. For most entertainment writers, however, dance is, at best, only an occasional subject for review.

Television changes so much that it is difficult to predict. There will be a time of heavy (and well-publicized) activity that produces the likes of "Roots," "Holocaust," "Shogun, " "The Winds of War," and "Amerika," followed by a return to predictable sitcoms, reruns, and athletic events.

What seems to be occupying entertainment writers much more than television is the increased interest in videos, which range in subject matter from a successful professional football team to an exercise video to the latest from a Michael Jackson. At one time it was difficult to find a house without a television set. Now it is almost as hard to find one without a videocassette recorder (VCR).

If architecture, sculpture, dance, and television are the occasional arts, then art, music, drama, film, and literature are the constants.

The exception to this "Big Five" comes when book reviews are handled by another section or person, such as a features editor or writer. The trend is for the entertainment writer to be familiar with these five, and to expect to get regular assignments from among them. This writer may specialize in one or more, but becoming familiar with all and learning to capitalize on the unusual or unique aspect of each, he is prepared to jump in any direction when the call comes.

Some Arts Are Seasonal

Artistic efforts do not spread themselves out conveniently through the week; they tend to collect on weekends; nor does the art scene grind to a halt when the reviewer is on vacation.

There are normally musical and dramatic seasons, when the entertainment staff is stretched thin. The same holds true for local or amateur art, which appears in warm-month festivals or fairs. A major traveling exhibit may come at any time, but that need not be a drain on the time of the entertainment staff.

When the treasures of King Tut's tomb were on tour visiting six major cities in the country, and when Art of the Vatican was making the rounds to a few select spots, they were thoroughly covered not only by national publications, but also by the wire services and various syndicates. Because these latter serve just about every newspaper in America, any editor could offer a qualified review without using his own people; or he could decide that the expense of a locally produced review was worth it, and send someone from his own staff.

Films and books require continual attention, but the difference is one of selectivity. Traditionally, there are spring and fall publishing schedules; and in film, the summer brings action, adventure, and romance to the screen, whereas the end of the year brings so-called "quality" or more serious fare in time for Academy Award consideration.

If there is a full-time reviewer on the staff of a small paper, he or she will probably specialize in movies. With the major releases, the kind of films normally nominated for the big awards, foreign films, and occasional documentaries, to say nothing of whatever the current exploitation genre is, there is always something new showing in town. The standard practice on most entertainment staffs is to review all new major releases, cover a foreign film or documentary if there is an unusual aspect to it or if it is a slow day otherwise, and ignore the rest.

Eric Gerber (personal communication, June, 1983), for years the main film writer for the *Houston Post*, finally put his foot down and announced that he would no longer review Kung Fu, teen-scream, soft porn, or Black exploitation movies. Neither editors nor readers seemed to mind, and those films kept on coming to Houston and doing as well as they ever had. It would seem that those who attend these attractions do not pay much attention to reviews anyway.

An Exception in Dallas

There was an intriguing situation at the *Dallas Times-Herald* in the early 1980s when an experimental column called "Joe Bob at the Drive-In," written by the paper's regular film expert under the name Joe Bob Briggs, became the most popular feature of the Friday issue. Joe Bob concentrated on drive-in fare, and regaled his readers with regular body-part counts and bare-breast tallies, as well as a sprinkling of rural opinion on any matter that came to mind. The column won friends and made enemies and was eventually banished from the newspaper, but only after attracting the attention of the prestigious *New Yorker* magazine and creating a reviewing legend that has become part of Texas folklore.[1]

Books are more constant than films, but again, there are too many titles to be covered by any one newspaper. Book reviews are usually the responsibility of a book editor, who may or may not have a connection with a features or entertainment desk. The standard practice is to farm out reviews, letting interested readers become regular reviewers in exchange for the book. The economics cannot be beat; the book is free, and so is the review. And sometimes the editor gets good copy

---

[1]*The New Yorker*, December 22, 1986.

at no cost. Admittedly, this is not the best way. Some book editors claim their regular outside reviewers are more qualified, on the basis of years of experience, than those in the building. Reporters and editors can and do write book reviews, but often find that the time involved is difficult to justify.

The Spontaneity of a Performing Art

In the performing arts, the viewer witnesses a live performance, even if it is on film or tape, and regardless of the rehearsal time or the number of takes. The same holds true for recorded music. With live theater and music there is no question of immediacy. The important distinction is not so much that the event is or was at one time spontaneous, but that the viewer has no control (with the exception of remote-controlled videocassettes) over the time of exposure and appreciation. The importance of this aspect of performing arts comes when the reviewer ventures an analysis. The writer must remember that the viewer controls his or her own time. If he or she looks away, that minute part of the performance is gone forever. Anyone's attention wanders, at least briefly, in all but the most gripping performances. The writer praises an activity that is appealing on a broad basis, and condemns that which relies on a small moment or act for its success.

One who appreciates the arts, sitting in a spectator's or a reviewer's seat, will form an opinion of an emotional activity, such as a performing art, sooner and more easily than with a passive act, a fine art. The audience at a performance must be ready to accept what is presented when it is presented. With the fine arts, the viewer first selects the time he or she wishes to enjoy the book, painting, sculpture, or building, and in addition, controls the amount of time to be spent with it. The entire mentality is different, and the reviewer must be aware of the difference. One might spend an entire evening marveling at Andrew Wyeth's "Helga" pictures, but when Placido Domingo is singing at the Met, you are there before the opening curtain or you miss an act. And he does not sing the role over if you happened to doze off during the evening.

Different Efforts, Different Approaches

The review of a performing art can take one of several different approaches. It can be explanatory, and attempt to educate as it informs; or it can assume, as so many reports on popular music do, that the reader is already knowledgeable.

The following review of a performance of "Boris Godunov" shows how a live performance can lead to explanation as well as criticism.[2] The language is basic, although the themes are complicated. Notice how the writer puts the opera into histor-

---

[2]Courtesy of the Sacramento *Bee*, November 25, 1983.

ical perspective, how he does some incidental educating by explaining the word "proster," and how he offers a mild reproach for casting a boy in the role of Feodor.

'BORIS GODUNOV': GRAND OPERA TREATMENT OF THE CZAR'S ERA

By Alfred Kay
Bee Reviewer

SAN FRANCISCO—No opera comes to mind more deserving of the adjective grand than "Boris Godunov," which Wednesday evening, and a good part of the night, re-entered the repertoire of the San Francisco Opera.

It is large in scope and score. It is poignant in its details of personal guilt but broad in the pageantry of a Czar's coronation and moribund reign.

Of all of its qualities, though, this current "Boris" should be noted for its inherent strength. And no wonder, for the orchestration is by Modest Mussorgsky himself, a compilation of the two versions which were rejected and ridiculed during the composer's lifetime. Later, of course, Rimsky-Korsakov was to turn a rough-hewn score into something lush and seamless, but here in evidence are all of the Russian's eccentricities and blatant blending of music and theater.

The general effect of this opera, then, might best be described by the Russian word proster. For this means space, but as much in its feeling as in square footage—the feeling of wonderment, say, in viewing the vast Siberian birch forests or Ukranian fields of wheat. And a production which runs more than four hours can certainly handle Mussorgsky's sort of proster.

Indeed, it takes some handling, for the production is the largest ever mounted by the San Francisco company. It took seven trailer trucks to transport the scenery from the Metropolitan Opera in New York, and it demands a chorus of 82 people, 40 supernumeraries, 40 stage hands and, it would seem, all the bells and trumpets that could be borrowed.

Notable, too, is the fact that the San Francisco cast is performing this classic in Russian, because other languages diminish some of the most dramatic scenes in all of opera. Boris suffocating in Italian, even if the Italian were Ezio Pinza, is not the same thing.

Everybody should therefore hear Nicolai Ghiaurov in the title role, for he is near perfection. Yet, it is ironic that in this rough-edged Mussorgsky version, we have a singer of uncommon refinement, more akin to the context of Rimsky-Korsakov. The great Fedor Chaliapin wrung out anguished words during the clock and death scenes, and Pinza, too, depended heavily on dramatic phrasing and incident. Ghiaurov is more musical, and his fine voice rises in quality as it rises above the orchestra and chorus, but the interpretation is excellent in its own way.

John Tomlinson as Pimen and Kevin Langan as the vagabond monk also displayed fine voices, though Wieslaw Ochman as the Pretender Dimitri and Stefka Mineva as Marina (replacing an ailing Tatiana Troyanos) added little to what, at best, are thankless roles.

In reflecting on "Boris," however, one is struck by the fact that the title role, so commanding and interesting, provides so very few moments on stage and how much of the opera is given over to the chorus. There are peasants milling everywhere, and even the very first scene belongs to them. It is consequently heartening to note that the 82 milling singers in this production were outstanding, and added grandeur and drama to the powerful tale that somebody has already described as "Czar Wars."

Also to be reflected upon is the uncommon use of a boy soprano in the role of Feodor, usually sung by an adult female, and I think that a case can be made both for and against the approach. Young Edmund Kimbell undeniably added a bit of freshness and authenticity to the scenes with his father Boris, but such a necessarily small voice, among so many large ones, can also be distracting, so one simply takes his choice.

Nobody, though, has to ponder the conducting of Marek Janjowsky and the sets, originally designed for the Metropolitan Opera, by Ming Cho Lee. Both evoked wonderfully the sights and sounds of old Russia—from the bells in the tower to the bricks of the Kremlin wall—so the entire production emerged with all the power and all the proster required for very grand opera.

By contrast, here is a review of a rock concert by the group Yes that would attract few readers outside those who regularly follow the popular music scene.[3] In fairness, this kind of performance seems to produce this kind of review, whether the event takes place in Cedar Rapids, Iowa, as this one did, or Sacramento. Phrases such as "expansive, metallic, oblong, clean and uncluttered" hold little meaning for those not familiar with this type of review. The typical practice seems to be to assume quite a bit of knowledge about the performers on the part of the reader, an approach that would be dangerous indeed with "Boris Godunov."

THIS ROCK GROUP DIFFERENT? YES!

By Dee Ann Rexroat
Gazette Staff Writer

The first band ever to play in the Five Seasons Center returned last night atop a crest of newfound popularity.

The British band Yes, recently regrouped after a three-year hiatus, led a crowd of 5,500 on an amazing two-hour session of musical acrobatics.

They opened the concert with a cappella five-part harmonies, their characteristically full and contrapuntal vocals filling the arena like a thick fog.

As was evident throughout the evening, Yes sacrifices record sales by rejecting the Top 40 formula of sing-along lyrics, simple melodies and A-B-A song structure. Proof of their musical integrity is the fact that before the break-up, they remained popular and influential for 12 years with only one major hit: "Roundabout"—the long-anticipated encore of the Five Seasons concert.

Even the guitar solos by new guitar recruit Trevor Rabin have no resemblance to the usually furious and predictable rock guitar solos. Rabin, original bassist Chris Squire and original keyboardist Tony Kaye all displayed melodic and technical grace throughout the concert.

An absolutely outstanding light and laser show dramatically interpreted the music

---

[3]Reprinted by permission of the Cedar Rapids *Gazette*, March 7, 1984.

of Yes, climaxing at the end of the concert with a column of lasers spelling out YES in three layers. The ultra-modern set also exemplified the music: expansive, metallic, oblong, clean and uncluttered.

Yes played a good mix of new and old repertoire, with some oldies repackaged into solos or presented in fragments. "Owner of a Lonely Heart," their current smash hit, was received with a short standing ovation by the happy crowd.

Lead singer Jon Anderson, referred to half-jokingly during the concert as "our newest member" (he is an original Yes member and the last to re-join), is a curiously stiff singer. His voice is penetrating but he looks as if he'll break if he makes a sudden movement.

The most colorful band member is bassist Squire. The biblical Joseph's coat of many colors couldn't compete with Squire's robe, made of silver satin with black and red fringes, fur and a blue heart patch with rhinestones.

Sometimes this "in the know" approach is intentional, sometimes it is not. The popular group Chicago, for instance, changed lead singers in the mid-1980s, and review after review mentioned the new member. None said where Peter Cetera went, if he still lived and performed, or why he departed. A random sampling of students showed that all already knew, and none seemed to feel that the reviews were incomplete because they made no mention of his current whereabouts.

A more important criticism of contemporary reviewers is that they may know perfectly well what they want to say—that is, there is nothing wrong with their ability to appreciate and criticize—but they have difficulty finding the exact words. This is the argument put forth by editors who would rather train a journalist to be a reviewer than teach an artist journalism. Supposedly, the journalist already has some familiarity with words and their effect. Many know more about the arts than the all-purpose reviewer, but unless they are able to express themselves, they are of no help to a newspaper. Reporters often learn the hard way the difference between what they meant to say and how their words were taken by readers.

Ask a college class to review an art, and most will choose film or television, not so much because of the preponderance of product, but because the beginner feels at home with them: "I don't know much about art, but I'm a real movie fan." The student will overlook the fact that, as a rule, the readers themselves are far more familiar with the plastic arts. The veteran writes with care about a familiar art, just because it is familiar.

The More Quiet Side of the Street

The fine arts present a different situation. Here, creativity has already taken place; the audience is present for the results of that creative effort.

The consumer can enjoy a fine art at his or her leisure, and can repeat, almost indefinitely, the experience. He or she re-reads a passage in a book, goes back for a second or third look at a painting, or views a well-placed piece of sculpture from every angle. There is no spontaneity of discovery, no fanfare, no quickening, no rush, no tears with this kind of artistic presentation. At the exact moment a statue is undraped, or a painting or an architect's sketch for a new building revealed, there may be some of that feeling, but the longer the exposure, the more distant that excitement of revelation becomes. Each person will impose his or her own time frame on his or her appreciation. No two people read at exactly the same rate, and no two people seeing a painting unveiled will look at exactly the same parts of it at the same time. Yet with the performing arts the audience is compelled to watch as the event unfolds, and the producers, not the viewers, control the time element.

Reviews of the fine arts tend to be more intellectual and less volatile than those of the performing arts, and the language found in them follows suit. This is not to suggest that the reviewer try to counter this basic tenet by trying to spice up copy on the fine arts, or downplay the excitement of the performing arts. Being aware of the difference should be enough.

Students often fall into this trap and try to make reviews of fine arts as exciting as those of performing arts. Their lack of familiarity and confidence shows as they tackle the fine arts. Here a student struggles with a book review:

Joseph Wambaugh's DELTA STAR

Joseph Wambaugh has assembled yet another collection of misfits and weirdos, given them police badges, and set them loose on the seedy streets of Los Angeles in his most recent book, The Delta Star. Their adventures, on- and off-duty, are totally captivating, and the novel is hard to put down.

While the focal point of Wambaugh's book seems to be his bizarre characters, one storyline, a homicide case, runs through the novel. A young hooker, Thelma Bernbaum (alias Missy Moonbeam), topples from the roof of her hotel, an apparent suicide.

"And that, Mario Villalobos had to agree, was a fitting epitaph for all the Thelma Bernbaums who ended up on a steel table in the coroner's by way of the streets of Hollywood: it ain't no big thing."

But burnt-out Homicide Detective Villalobos discovers the opposite—it is a big thing. He is led on a twisting investigative path that encompasses a dead private eye, a gay murder target, the California Institute of Technology, the Nobel Prize Committee, immortality, and his personal self-discovery.

Though the homicide case is certainly interesting, Wambaugh's forte is characterization. His oddball cops come alive with personalities of their own, put a stranglehold on the readers' sympathies and never let go. They are shown as jaded and cynical, as idealistic and vulnerable. They project rays of camaraderie and streaks of disdain. They find out about themselves and their co-workers by sharing the horror, violence, dirt and grit of L.A.

The cast includes Jane "Wayne," the Amazon punk rocker, "Rambling Ronald," who is counting the minutes until he's eligible for his pension, K-9 cop Hans and his ferocious Rottweiler, Ludwig, Dilford and Dolly, the "Personality Team" who don't get along, and Bad Czech, the biggest, meanest cop in the division, who is slightly demented, icy cold, and in one touching scene, extremely caring and vulnerable. Lording over this misfit troop is Leery, owner of The House of Misery, who pours double shots to the cops drowning the frustrations of police work and trying to forget about spiked babies and paws in petunias.

The Delta Star is fast-paced, realistic and entertaining. Wambaugh can be both witty and grim without being melodramatic. He pulls the reader into the world of his characters, providing 291 pages of sheer entertainment.

This student made two major errors, each traceable to his lack of familiarity with a static art. First, there are glaring cliches (the novel is hard to put down, 291 pages of sheer entertainment), and second, there is the assumption that the reader knows all about Wambaugh and his books. At the very beginning the writer credits the assembly of "yet another collection of misfits," and the reader may not be aware of any previous such collections. This book review seems to fit the form of a review of a long-running television series, or of a widely publicized film that is a sequel to an earlier success. In those instances it is fairly safe to assume some audience familiarity. In a book, even from a popular and successful writer like Joseph Wambaugh, it is not.

However, the real problem with this review is that the writer did not stop to put into perspective the differences between a performing and a fine art. He approached the book review as he would a film or television review and tried to recreate what he mistakenly saw as spontaneous creativity. His language reflects that approach. This difference in language, however, reflecting the difference between a fine and a performing art, can also be the difference between a successful and an unsuccessful review.

When you are at the symphony, you should be stimulated as powerful chords of great music fill the hall. At the same time, the reader enjoying the genius of a Nobel Prize-winning author in the quiet of his living room is also moved, but in a different, less dramatic way. This is how writing about these events should be considered. It is necessary to understand the difference in word choice between a fine and a performing art; to understand the difference between what could be called spontaneous and delayed or unobserved creativity; to understand that readers will feel a natural familiarity with the performing arts and usually some distance from the fine arts. Then the reviewer, and the review, is off to a good start.

Chapter Three
A Method for Reviewing the Arts

"The Roar of the Greasepaint—The Smell of the Crowd!", that is where the action is, and where the excitement and recognition lie, not in laying out pages, writing headlines, making photo assignments or checking television logs. Who does not envy the writer who numbers among his associates the glamorous and the famous, in addition to less-exciting entities such as fellow reporters, copyeditors, and photographers. Many feel that those who work with sports and politics do so primarily to satisfy some vicarious urge. Those who serve on the arts-entertainment-amusements staffs exist, at least peripherally, in show biz.

Little wonder, then, that the entertainment desk staffer prefers to think of himself as a reviewer, and chooses not to quarrel with those who label him *critic*. It is the chance to pass judgment on new and old works, to serve as an artistic watchdog for the community, and to test his evaluative abilities and to measure them against others that attracts the reporter to the features or amusements department. Because the critic probably followed a different path to reach her level of comment on the arts, probably through performance or at least a period of college-level specialization, this discussion concentrates on the entertainment writer as reviewer. However, an analysis of both reviews and criticisms shows that each will normally follow the same format, or method. The approach to the job may vary, but the form of the results will be similar.

Looking for Common Elements in the Arts

The writer new to the job may know a lot about the newspaper business, and may have some association with one or more of the performing or fine arts. However, without a method of some sort to follow he is likely to make the mistake of imitating his predecessor. But the best writing is original, not imitative.

One may start with the intention of writing a review, but it may turn out to be more of a report if the writer is on unfamiliar ground. A report is an objective account of an event. With opinion it becomes a review, and in-depth analysis makes it a criticism. This is an oversimplification, but serves as a starting point because the key to successful reviewing or criticizing is being able to define and comment on creativity. Perhaps the next step is to understand that most artistic efforts are neither all good nor all bad. The average review is mixed in that there is something to praise and something to regret. Good writing makes the review or criticism generally positive, or generally negative. Just because the orchestra is playing Beethoven does not mean the performance is automatically successful, or just because the New York Philharmonic is on the stage does not guarantee a great evening of music.

The new-at-the-task reviewer can make his job considerably easier by following a basic method. It will provide him a framework for his reactions to a performance, and will prepare him for the fateful day when the boss says "The ballet is in town, and you're going to cover it."

THE FIVE-PART REVIEW

Successful reviews seem to have five common elements, and all the beginning writer need do is to see that each is present in the review, and he will be off to a good start. With practice the method becomes automatic, just as adding necessary attribution to a news story becomes routine for the general assignment reporter.

The five parts of the review are a strong opening, a strong closing, identification, summary, and opinion. In one way or another, the huge majority of acceptable, successful reviews will incorporate them. They are, in effect, the Five W's of reviewing.

A Strong Opening and Closing

The opening is critical in that it must attract a reader's attention, and at the same time give some indication as to the success of the event being reviewed. A bland opening will send a reader to another story as quickly as a news story with a weak lead. The review that begins "The orchestra presented a Beethoven concert last night" has as much journalistic merit as the lead that says "The City Council met last night." A lead that has been borrowed and abused far too often is the one that reads "The orchestra played Beethoven last night; Beethoven lost." Although this is also an example of "wise guy" writing at its worst, it is nevertheless a strong opening statement.

Here's how Janna Anderson began a negative movie review:[1] "Plotless. Action-less. Directionless. Pointless. That's 'Breathless'." Sometimes the short, catchy lead is best, more often than not when the opinion is going to be negative. At other times a milder approach is effective.

The *Sacramento Bee*[2] handled a roundup of several current films this way: " 'Uncommon Valor' is a strong and likeable adventure movie about a group of Vietnam veterans returning to Southeast Asia to rescue some of their buddies left behind 10 years ago." And: " 'Gorky Park' is a faithful adaptation of the novel by Martin Cruz Smith with a dazzling performance by William Hurt as the Moscow detective. Despite that, the movie fails." And still another: " 'The Man Who Loved Women' has to be the flattest movie I've ever seen, a boring mess with Burt Reynolds so lifeless you wonder why he bothers to make these films in which he tries to emulate Cary Grant—and fails every time." In each of these instances the reader knows immediately what the reviewer's general reaction is, which makes them strong leads.

In the last example, the writer injects himself into the lead, a questionable and even dangerous practice. If the writer is widely known it can be effective; if not it can be taken as arrogance. The test should be this: When the reader picks up the newspaper, and perhaps reports on it to a friend, does that reader say "The *Times* loved it," or "Atkinson loved it?" At some point the reviewer, or critic, earns the right to use the first person in a review. Common sense suggests that the writer should not rush to establish his own name; better to concentrate on writing good, consistent reviews. The accolades will come in time. When the ads begin to say "Atkinson of the *Times* loved it," rather than "The *Times* loved it," the writer is on his way. When the ad says "Atkinson: I loved it," he has arrived.

The good review, in itself a piece of writing worthy of comment, will also have a strong closing statement that reflects the sentiment expressed in the opening. This closing comes either in the final paragraph, or in the next-to-last one when some information about curtain time or ticket availability concludes the piece. No better illustration of this can be found than in the Atkinson review that appears later in this chapter.

Identification

In between the opening and the close, the writer must include identification, summary, and opinion. Identification poses few problems—the current trend seems to be to write "now playing at neighborhood theaters" for films, or indicating the channel, rather than the network, for television. Identification for the fine arts, as well as dance, drama, and music, consists primarily of location. Although this would seem to be the easiest—and perhaps the most mechanical—part of the review, there

---

[1]Courtesy of The Fargo *Forum*, Fargo, ND–Moorhead, MN, May 17, 1983.
[2]Courtesy of the Sacramento *Bee*, December 16, 1983.

are pitfalls. Identification must include enough information for the reader of the review to find the film, play, or exhibit, know what time it begins, how long it will be around, who is selling it, perhaps how easy or difficult it is to see. But there should also be no doubt about the type of effort being reviewed. When the novice writes " 'Manon' is a truly moving experience," the reader does not know if the review is about a book, television program, film, play or, as it turns out, none of the above.

The most common practice among reviewers is to divide identification, putting the name of the work and its principal contributor or creator at the top, and adding such other necessary information later, often as part of a strong closing statement. Just don't let the reader (or editor) ever ask, "What am I reading about?" Actually, the task of identification is considerably easier on many newspapers where the practice is to include such information in a box within or beside the review itself.

Summary Is not Synopsis

Summary is a problem in reviewing films, television, drama, or literature, because too many writers think it is the same thing as synopsis. It isn't. Synopsis is a blow-by-blow, chronological account of an event that contains a story line. By definition, a *synopsis* starts at the beginning and is, in effect, a capsule of the action. The synopsis is appropriate in a serial story and takes the form of "in our story so far." That is not a summary. Yet, writers unwilling to work at their craft consider a review of a film, television program, or play to be a lead followed by synopsis, with opinion thrown in from time to time.

The summary does not automatically include the locale or time of the action, and it does not need to include every role or all performers. The summary says, simply, what the play, book, film, or program is about.

A successful television series such as "The Cosby Show" has been summarized in every major publication, and can serve as a model for writers looking for an example. Each episode can also be used to summarize the entire series. A review of a typical episode could begin "As the action begins Theo is on the telephone trying to convince his buddy Cockroach that they need summer jobs. Cliff Huxtable enters, followed by daughters Rudi and Vanessa, and asks Theo how long he plans to be on the phone." And so on. That is not a summary. It would be better to write "Thursday's 'Cosby' episode is based on Dad Cliff's long-running plan to get son Theo in college, and Theo's equally long-running interest in girls." In the case of a highly successful series such as this, and "M*A*S*H" and "I Love Lucy" before it, the writer can assume some familiarity with the series on the part of his readers.

Opinion

Opinion is a little more difficult than might be apparent at first, particularly in the case of the review, because the writer must not stop at saying something is good or bad, but why it is good or bad. Unfortunately some critics, even those with legitimate credentials, feel it is enough for them to proclaim something good or bad, and that is reason enough in itself. That attitude, unfortunately, does nothing to diminish the impression of arrogance that many critics are charged with.

Expressing an opinion is a natural thing to do in a free society, but when it comes to the reviewer, it is complicated because there must be support. It is not enough to like or dislike something; there must be reasons why. In the instance of the reviewer, charged with expressing opinion about a number of the arts, it will help to develop some idea of what makes a film successful, a book interesting, a play inspiring, a rock concert exciting. The writer learns to use these qualities as the basis for his judgment. Actors should be believable. Musicians should be adept on their instruments. Singers should have good tone and sing within their ranges, authors should understand their subjects, dancers should be graceful and well-rehearsed, painters and sculptors should demonstrate skill with hands and materials.

The review should be a subjective appraisal, but what to do when the writer does not feel qualified to express an opinion? This happens often with the fine arts; new reviewers seem most at home and more willing to comment on the performing arts. More than one writer, faced with modern painting, sculpture, or poetry, has yielded to the temptation to write a report, or has minimally satisfied the requirements of the review through such words as "pleasant," "interesting," "intriguing," or "provocative." Sometimes, it seems, that is the best that can be done. Another way out is to comment on what an audience finds most interesting, or in the event of a competition, borrow from the judges' language. But these are stopgap measures. Experience should bring familiarity enough so that the review writer becomes as comfortable with modern art as he does with modern music.

Start Off with Opinion

Opinion starts in the lead, in the form of a word or phrase. Some identification usually follows, then summary, then more identification. Once the tone has been set, opinion can be expressed throughout by a carefully selected adjective or adverb, with examples where appropriate. Most reviews are constructed this way, but there is too much variety within and among the arts to attempt to develop a rigid formula. The closest one comes is to suggest a strong opening and close, and appropriate identification, opinion, and summary.

Brooks Atkinson's review of the first performance of Arthur Miller's "Death of a Salesman" serves as an example of how an overnight review should be written. Although Atkinson reached such an exalted state as a New York critic that a Broadway theater was named after him, he still was responsible for producing an immediate reaction to an artistic effort, just as any small-town reviewer would. To set the scene:

It was widely known in New York in late 1948 that a new Arthur Miller play was in rehearsal. Miller already had an excellent reputation as one of the nation's leading new playwrights, and Atkinson was well established as the *New York Times'* principal drama critic. Advertisements were appearing in the newspaper by February of 1949, heralding the new play. On February 6, the Sunday before the play was to open in New York, the *Times* carried at the top of its theater page a drawing of the main actors and a one-sentence summary of the plot. On that day Atkinson had devoted his Sunday space to a discussion of the musical "Carousel," and expressed the opinion that it was destined to become one of the great productions in the history of the musical theater.

A Review a Night, Even for the Critic

It was a busy time on Broadway, and on Wednesday evening, February 9, Atkinson attended the premiere of a new two-act play called "My Name Is Aquilon." His review of that effort appeared in the *Times* the next morning, and that night "Death of a Salesman" opened. In other words, during that week in 1949, even though he continued to use his considerable critical gifts to produce his Sunday criticisms, he functioned primarily as a reviewer. It was rush to the theater, rush back to the office, and knock out a review.

This is what he wrote:[3]

DEATH OF A SALESMAN

By Brooks Atkinson

Arthur Miller has written a superb drama. From every point of view "Death of a Salesman," which was acted at the Morosco last evening, is rich and memorable drama. It is so simple in style and so inevitable in theme that it scarcely seems like a thing that has been written and acted. For Mr. Miller has looked with compassion into the hearts of some ordinary Americans and quietly transferred hope and anguish to the theatre. Under Elia Kazan's masterly direction, Lee J. Cobb gives a heroic performance, and every member of the cast plays like a person inspired. Two seasons ago Mr. Miller's "All My Sons" looked like the work of an honest and able playwright. In comparison with the new drama, that seems like a contrived play now. For "Death of a Salesman" has the flow and spontaneity of a suburban epic that may not be intended as poetry but becomes poetry in spite of itself because Mr. Miller has drawn it out of so many intangible sources.

It is the story of an aging salesman who has reached the end of his usefulness on the road. There has always been something unsubstantial about his work. But suddenly the unsubstantial aspects of it overwhelm him completely. When he was young, he looked dashing; he enjoyed the comradeship of other people—the humor, the kidding, the business.

---

[3]Copyright, 1949, by the *New York Times* Company. Reprinted by permission.

In his early sixties he knows his business as well as he ever did. But the unsubstantial things have become decisive; the spring has gone from his step, the smile from his face and the heartiness from his personality. He is through. The phantom of life has caught up with him. As literally as Mr. Miller can say it, dust returns to dust. Suddenly there is nothing.

This is only a little of what Mr. Miller is saying. For he conveys this elusive tragedy in terms of simple things—the loyalty and understanding of his wife, the careless selfishness of his two sons, the sympathetic devotion of a neighbor, the coldness of his former boss' son—the bills, the car, the tinkering around the house. And most of all: the illusions by which he has lived—opportunities missed, wrong formulas for success, fatal misconceptions about his place in the scheme of things.

Writing like a man who understands people, Mr. Miller has no moral precepts to offer and no solutions of the salesman's problems. He is full of pity, but he brings no piety to it. Chronicler of one frowzy corner of the American scene, he evokes a wraithlike tragedy out of it that spins through the many scenes of his play and gradually envelops the audience.

As theatre "Death of a Salesman" is no less original than it is as literature. Jo Mielziner, always equal to an occasion, has designed a skeletonized set that captures the mood of the play and serves the actors brilliantly. Although Mr. Miller's text may be diffuse in form, Mr. Kazan has pulled it together into a deeply moving performance.

Mr. Cobb's tragic portrait of the defeated salesman is acting of the first rank. Although it is familiar and folksy in the details, it has something of the grand manner in the big size and deep tone. Mildred Dunnock gives the performance of her career as the wife and mother—plain of speech but indomitable in spirit. The parts of the thoughtless sons are extremely well played by Arthur Kennedy and Cameron Mitchell, who are all youth, brag and bewilderment.

Other parts are well played by Howard Smith, Thomas Chalmers, Don Keefer, Alan Hewitt and Tom Pedi. If there were time, this report would gratefully include all the actors and fabricators of illusion. For they all realize that for once in their lives they are participating in a rare event in the theatre. Mr. Miller's elegy in a Brooklyn sidestreet is superb.

Although this was written decades ago it can still serve as a model for reviewers. The habit of referring to all persons as "Mr." was the way the *Times* did things then, whether the person in question was a playwright, a politician or an accused felon. The use of the verb "acted" in the second sentence, as well as the reference to "last evening" is vintage Atkinson and a little archaic for contemporary tastes; otherwise, the review holds up well. It begins with a strong opening statement, "Arthur Miller has written a superb drama," which is reflected in the closing, "Mr. Miller's elegy in a Brooklyn sidestreet is superb." Repeating the word "superb" for effect may not have been a conscious decision, but using the word "unsubstantial" three times in the third and fourth paragraphs was intentional and effective.

The identification is easy in this review, and handled intelligently. "At the Morosco" gives the where, and the rest of the review adequately covers the who and what. The third paragraph is a model of dramatic summary: "It is the story of an aging salesman who has reached the end of his usefulness on the road.'' Nothing could be clearer or more precise.

Whether it was intentional, there is a certain ranking here. Atkinson surely knew that his first mention of a person would set the tone for the review, and this would be critical to his overall evaluation. In those fleeting moments between the close of the play and the time he took his seat at the typewriter he had to decide how to begin. He would have had some idea before the play opened, because he was familiar with the work of Miller, Cobb, and Kazan. He selected Miller, who thus received more space in the review than the others. Quite clearly, Atkinson felt that these three dominated the production, because it is not until the seventh (of nine) paragraph that anyone else is named.

Analyzing the work of experts after the fact can be revealing. This review, in retrospect, showed exactly how the writer felt about the main contributors to the evening. With experienced writers, this kind of grading becomes second nature. Beginners will get in trouble if they try to rely too heavy on formulas or word count, or if they spend too much time analyzing their own work. Writing reviews and criticisms is in itself a form of creative activity, and creativity should be a natural, not a forced or programmed, activity.

One lesson that comes across clearly from this examination is that the person mentioned first in the review is the one the writer feels is most important, or most responsible. After that first mention there should be some balance among the elements the writer feels are important. If the reviewer decides, for example, that writer and actor should share the praise or blame, one is mentioned first, then the other follows, but gets a little more space.

This method, or any method, is only valuable if it feels comfortable to the writer. He is dealing with creative expressions, and it would be wrong to saddle him with too many rules or guidelines. But he will find most success if he makes sure his piece contains identification, summary, and opinion, and has strong opening and closing statements.

Chapter Four

Film—Where Everyone is an Expert

The beginning all-purpose reviewer, particularly one already employed at a newspaper, may want to test his new interest with film, arguably the most familiar of the arts and, with television, certainly the most popular. Television offerings vary as years go by, but probably there is little on the small screen calling for the reviewer's (or critic's) attention. Film is a good place to start.

Although the impact of television has been well documented as a result of royal weddings, political conventions, and Olympic games, many have forgotten what film has done to the civilized world. The splendid English actor Laurence Olivier in 1948 undertook the filming of Shakespeare's classic "Hamlet," and the film was a popular and critical success. It is still regarded as a masterpiece. After it had been in release for 6 months or so, more people had seen "Hamlet" on screen than had witnessed every live production since the play was written almost 400 years earlier. Or, more than half of the play's total audience going back 4 centuries had been chalked up in 6 months.

Film historians point to the effect the classic "Birth of a Nation" had on American viewers, and show how it was studied by the Russians and later the Germans as they saw the potential of film as a propaganda vehicle. Film has been, and will continue to be, not only a popular, but a powerful and persuasive medium.

The reviewer should begin his study of film by taking note of what is currently popular. Around the early 1980s, for example, the movie-going public was entranced by the special effects that added so greatly to the success of "Star Wars," "Star Trek—The Movie," "Close Encounters of the Third Kind," and "2001." But the fascination quickly paled, so much so that by the time the sequel "2010" appeared, there were very few new special space craft effects. It had become, for the moment, impossible to create something the audience had not seen.

However, during this time, film makers were capitalizing on something else—the sequel itself. Rambo and Rocky re-cloned themselves almost ad infinitum, as did the "Halloween" and "Friday the 13th" crowds.

STARTING AT THE TOP

The reviewer begins his assignment by taking note of the title of the film, an obvious but not always automatic move. The reviewer must never begin with the assumption that the reader knows what he is writing about—such as referring to "Steven Speilberg's latest" or "the current Molly Ringwald starrer"—when he has not given the complete, correct title. This is the worst sin of all, a kind of "in" writing where only friends of the reviewer, or those in the business, or those on the inside of a joke, know what the reference refers to.

Neither critic nor reviewer should force the reader to beg for information. Readers are not beggars, they are page turners, which is what they will do if treated in this high-handed manner.

Next may come a kind of description of the story, how the reviewer categorizes it, perhaps based on the acting, or the writing, or the directing. But the reviewer's label must not be a blind repeating of what the studio calls it. Hollywood may proclaim it as an "actor's film," or a "director's film." The promoters are attempting, in thus describing films, to call attention to what they feel is the most defensible aspect of a film or, if the truth be known, probably the part that cost the most money. When a widely known actor receives a salary in the millions of dollars, the studio heralds the epic as an actor's film, and if it is the effort immediately following an Academy Award for directing, the director will be labeled the big attraction. The most obvious way for a studio to do this is to put the name of the actor or director above the title, as in "Stephen King's 'Children of the Corn' " or "Robert Redford in 'The Natural'." But it is not up to the studios to tell the world what kind of film it is. The reviewer arrives at a decision based on what he has seen, not on what he has been told.

Still, it is probable that the leading actors, at least, will draw some prominent mention, if for no other reason than that the viewing public normally thinks of films in terms of actors, rather than directors or writers. Perhaps actors would not be mentioned in a documentary, where the people on the screen are not truly actors, or in a large cast full of screen newcomers in a low-budget movie, but even here at least some should be identified.

Again, as Hollywood periodically trots out new faces in some kind of exploitation film or other, the reviewer, feeling many will never be seen again, will skip the introductions. Indeed, the young actor Steve Guttenberg got his start in two such "teen-pop" films, "Police Academy" and "Police Academy II." Then he announced that he would not appear in another sequel, and turned his efforts to films where writing and direction were given more prominence.

Actor Robert Duvall produced a wonderful film called "Angelo, My Love" in which all but two minor players were unknown gypsies. Including all the names in a review would have added nothing; in fact, it would have given the impression that those named were actors. They weren't; they were people being themselves.

There are some films that do not get reviews in most of the nation's press, perhaps because they are foreign, or low-budget exploitation. But when the prerelease hype or promotion is such that the writer feels his readers want to know about a film, or when the film has been featured in full-page advertisements, it is almost mandatory to write something about it. The newspaper must be aware of reader curiosity, whether the product that caused it is noteworthy or not.

It Doesn't Always Work That Way

Still there are times when good intentions backfire. Years ago a soft-core pornography film was playing in Columbus, Ohio, and drawing very few customers. It was due to leave after a week or so of a remarkably unsuccessful run. For some reason a writer for a local paper decided that it should be sent packing with his own anger in hot pursuit. Thus he reviewed it, called it a waste of time, money, and effort, and said it was too lewd and obscene to warrant anyone's attention.

The next day the theater owner took out huge newspaper ads heralding "The Film They Said You Couldn't See." Box office input boomed, and the movie stuck around for an additional 6 months. It made its producers, as well as the theater owner, considerably richer than they had been, and all because of a misplaced effort on the part of one reviewer. Had this writer only said to himself "It's a lousy show, but at least it's leaving town," and left it at that, the story would have been different.

The safest way for the beginner to handle film reviews is to build a lead on actor, director, or story. The reviewer decides which is the strongest element in the success or failure of the show, and starts from there. This usually produces a strong opening statement, offers some early opinion, and gets the review off to a good start.

Here is how one student dealt with actors, story, and director.

Terms of Endearment

You laugh to keep from crying, and cry because you can't help it.

And when it's over, the characters in "Terms of Endearment" aren't the only ones who come to terms with life in general and family relationships in particular.

Nominated for 11 Academy Awards, including Best Film and Best Actress, and showing at local General Cinema theaters, "Terms of Endearment" is about the up-and-down, not always happy, 30-year relationship between a mother and her daughter.

It's a movie about love and learning how to express love. It's about maturing and changing and coming to grips with what is really important in life. And it is a first-class movie that will make even sour pusses smile and stern men wipe their eyes more than once during the two-and-a-half-hour film.

Aurora Greenway is the straight-laced, staid, frigid, lonely mother, played by Shirley

MacLaine, who not only finds her identity by the end of the movie, but also discovers contentment and some direction for her life.

Debra Winger plays Emma Greenway Horton, and she is anything but her mother's daughter. Emma is warm and honest and tolerates her mother's quirks, loving her regardless of their different outlooks on life.

The "boy" next door, Garrett Breedlove, is played by Jack Nicholson. A former American astronaut, he is a philandering, pot-bellied, happy-go-lucky "hero" who spends his days and nights chasing the bottle and younger skirts. And he does it well. For a nice realistic touch, Nicholson gained 30 pounds, and his pot belly is for real, always hanging out of his carelessly unbuttoned shirts or over his saggy swimming trunks.

All three, MacLaine, Winger and Nicholson, are nominated for Oscars for their impressive performances in "Terms of Endearment," but Nicholson is the only one who has an award under his belt. MacLaine has been nominated four times before and Winger once.

The high point of the film is the excellent, well-executed development of the three main characters. MacLaine successfully runs the gamut of emotions, evolving from a reserved, conservative River Oaks socialite to a heartwarming, mature woman who discovers what it is like to live and love fully. Overshadowed to some extent by MacLaine's dynamic role, Winger delivers a more subtle performance, but one that just cries for an empathetic response from the audience. And the lecherous Nicholson is disgusting, comical and completely endearing by the end of the movie.

The screenplay was written by James L. Brooks, who also produced and directed the movie. While the overall effect was good, at times Brooks condensed the 30-year time span too quickly and without enough transition between scenes.

At the beginning of the movie, Winger, in four consecutive scenes, ages from an infant to a young woman about to be married. And later, Winger's three children are born only a few scenes apart, reducing the impact of the event and causing a feeling of fragmentation.

But in the end, Brooks has a real winner, and the minor problems with transition are reconciled in the final scenes. The last half hour of the movie flows from scene to scene, as the movie winds down to a heartwrenching, but at the same time heartwarming ending. All three characters come to terms with their feelings, their relationships to other people and the paths that their lives have each taken.

It's touching, but not hokey, realistic but not too graphic. And you'll walk away with a warm, tingly feeling in your stomach, even if you aren't a mother or a daughter.

The weakness in this review is that it deals with generalities rather than specifics, and the reviewer's case is stronger if supported by concrete, rather than abstract, examples. It also lacks a strong opening statement giving some indication of the writer's evaluation. It is not until the fourth paragraph that there is a positive endorsement. The third paragraph combines summary and additional identification nicely, but the writer falls down later in proclaiming the high point to be the "well-executed development of the three main characters." This is probably a matter of terminology; a high point refers to a specific time during the film, and the writer meant that the strength of the film as a whole was the development of the actors. However, it ends nicely.

This review could be improved by moving opinion higher, such as: "You laugh to keep from crying, and cry because you just can't help it. And when it's over, the characters in 'Terms of Endearment,' which well deserves its 11 Academy Award nominations, aren't the only ones who come to terms with life in general and family relationships in particular."

The writer quickly learns that any mention of violence or sex or sensation or gore—the screen honey that attracts viewers like flies to a ripe peach—will add to the audience of a film whether the review is positive or negative. The best thing to do if the writer is convinced that the film is worthless trash—and this decision should be shared with a superior, either in the entertainment department or with the newspaper's editor—is to ignore it. But again, this raises the question about the reviewer's responsibility to his readers. In a way it is a can't win situation; the newspaper ignores the "come-on" ads and the readers wonder why. The newspaper says the film is trash, and the trash-seekers flock to the theater.

Where to Put the Blame

The Director

Often films are bad because the direction is bad. Normally the director's name is included as part of basic identification, and whether he figures in the opinion is up to the writer and the particular film. If space allows and the review is positive the director should be mentioned, but the reviewer must remember that most of his readers know acting, and relate to actors, and tend to judge a film on the basis of the people on the screen. The exception is if the director is very well known, or has had a recent honor.

Once past the name of the film, principal actors, and director, the list of elements in the film becomes optional. The experienced reviewer will mentally click off, as he watches, those areas that are worthy of mention, and those that are not.

When a film is spectacularly successful, it is because many of the behind-the-scenes folk have done such a superb job that their efforts go unnoticed by the general public. The costumer, film editors, lighting and sound people, for example; if their work is perfect, as is the case with sensitive direction, the viewer is not aware of it. The reviewer may choose to concentrate on acting and directing, plus perhaps writing, and often will not mention the fine points that made the film successful. Is this right? Doesn't this mislead the reader into thinking that acting and directing are everything?

There is no obvious answer. After all, how many people go to see a film because of the hair dresser, or makeup artist, or assistant second unit director? The answer, outside of immediate families, is none. People go to see stars, directors, stories and, perhaps, special effects or music. They expect the writer to concentrate on these elements. But the skilled and conscientious reviewer will try to add a little to each review. He will spend most of his time on the main points, but as time allows, and particularly if he is able to write in-depth analyses for a Sunday or weekend edition, he will do some educating about the less visible, but vital, aspects of film making.

One thing the reviewer can do, to make peace with his own conscience, is to consider that the craftsmen in the business—set designers, carpenters, editors, property managers—are inclined to be paid on the basis of their experience (to say nothing of their unions), rather than on the success of a film, whereas the actors' and director's salaries may be based on the public's acceptance of their work.

The Mysterious Producer

Producers are an interesting breed. Some are purely money people; they offer their own funds, or raise funds through others, hire a director, then sit back and await the results. They may be in the business only to make money, or they may have all the money they need and just like the idea of promoting art through films. Given the conglomerate nature of most of America's businesses today, the producer may well be primarily an agent for a holding company. Some, however, take a far more active part and demand approval of virtually everything, including casting, location, shooting schedule and, of course, budget. It is all but impossible for the average film-goer to ascertain the extent of the producer's role.

The reviewer, armed with publicity releases from the studio, has a clearer idea. Each day his mail includes packages from film people, and he regularly reads wire stories from Hollywood and gossip columnists, so he has some idea as to the role of the producer in a certain film. The producer may also direct, which makes the task of identifying responsibility even easier. Some producers are known by the type of film they are associated with—violent, or sex or message films—and deserve mention accordingly. On occasion, a producer makes a radical departure from the type of film he or she is associated with and undertakes something completely different. In this instance it is crucial to name the producer, particularly if the film is successful.

Perhaps the worst thing any one writer can do is to dutifully repeat what the studio says: "A John Smith production of a James Smith film based on a Julius Smith story adapted for the screen by Jerry Smith and presented by John Jones." Such studio drivel is absolutely meaningless to a reader, and does not deserve valuable newspaper space.

Whose Idea Was It?

The Writer

The source of a film can be an important or an incidental part of a review. Scripts written expressly for the screen may need to be judged differently from adaptions of stage plays or books. The adaption from page to screen may have been done to take advantage of the new medium, or it may be that too much of the excellence of the original has been lost. Some say it is impossible to move a story intact from one medium to another, yet "Death of a Salesman" moved fairly easily from stage to screen, then even to television. "Music Man" was another stage-to-screen success story. But critics were disappointed in the failure of a screen version of "A Chorus Line," although the unhappiness was due more to changes in the script than in moving to another medium. Considerably earlier, "From Here To Eternity" as a movie earned plaudits to equal those awarded the book; yet the movie was based on only part of the great book. The fascinating prison section in the middle was left out of the film version.

Perhaps the strangest transition from one medium to another had to do with the sociological study "Sex and the Single Girl," a nonfiction best-selling series of interviews in print. On the screen the only resemblance was the name. Hollywood came up with a story, capitalized on the title, and made a few bucks. A close second in this category would be the 1987 television film called "Breaking Home Ties" that was based on a 1954 *Saturday Evening Post* cover by Norman Rockwell. *Time* magazine suggested that a three-part mini-series called "American Gothic," based on Grant Wood's painting, could be next.

If a Nobel Prize-winning author is adapting his own work for the screen, that is surely worth writing about. But if the film is what is called an exploitation film— capitalizing on whatever is popular among theater audiences, perhaps violence, or medical shows, or Kung Fu artists—and has been hastily thrown together before the public loses interest, the source is incidental. The writer needs to identify the source, then decide how important it is to the review.

Film makers like to think of themselves as occupying a place in history, whether the rest of the industry or the viewing public sees them that way. They will present themselves as creators, as originators, as artists, as conceptualizers par excellence. It is the newspaper writer's job to put them in their proper perspective, to tell his readers how much is originality and how much is imitation.

It takes time and study to develop this aspect of reviewing, but it eventually becomes a most important part of the task. This goes right back to the basics of journalism. The entertainment writer tries to present all sides of an issue, whereas the studio releasing an expensive film will present only those aspects that enhance it.

For example, a sequel is not necessarily based on the soundness of the idea of the original, but rather on the box office receipts. Identifying a sequel is usually easy, as evidenced by "Jaws," "Jaws II," "Rocky," "Rocky II," "Rocky III," "Star Wars," "The Empire Strikes Back," "Return of the Jedi," and so forth. In other instances the reviewer or critic should mention similar efforts, such as an earlier Hollywood version of "Beau Geste," or "For Whom the Bell Tolls." Because the producers and directors see themselves in some historical perspective, so should the writers regard them. This also comes under the heading of educating the reader.

As an illustration, the people who came up with the "Airport" films were not really original thinkers. That series had its beginnings in the old "Grand Central Station" of film and radio, and in truth the concept goes back to the 14th century with Chaucer, and probably before. Again, the popular comedy "Ruthless People" was based on a bizarre kidnaping scheme that came right out of O. Henry's classic short story, "The Ransom of Red Chief."

These newcomers were imitators, which is not necessarily bad, but they were not creators in the sense that they developed an original concept. In writing reviews, writers can ask such questions as these: Would the considerable success of "The Magnificent Seven" have been possible without the frequent mention of the Samurai tradition that served as its basis? Would the popular "Victor, Victoria" have been as readily accepted without the reminder that it was based on a much earlier German version? If the writer decides that the film has merit on its own, he should say so. But if he similarly decides that the frequent mention of earlier generations adds to the overall effect, he should mention that, too. Probably the best way to handle this, considering the prerelease promotion, is to decide what the average movie-goer knows about the film, and figure that into the review. These are once again elements for the reviewer to consider, not to routinely include or exclude from his writing. The secret of successful reviewing, whether performed by reviewer or critic, is first to learn or to take into account all possible reasons for the success or failure of an effort, then be able to distinguish which contributed and which did not.

Checking Out the Where and the When

The location of the action of a film and the period when the action took place are high on the list of matters probably to be included. There are instances where they are not a factor, but normally the reviewer sets the scene for the action, as well as the time—past, future, contemporary, and so forth. But there is danger out there in Bijou-land for the unsuspecting. A story may be set in a certain location, but that does not mean it was filmed there. A second unit might have gone to the actual site to film exterior scenes, while the bulk of the action was filmed on Hollywood sound stages.

A film's historical accuracy is another problem for the viewer and the reviewer. The studio's promotion department will indicate that what goes on on the screen is what went on in life—few studios cheerfully admit to taking flagrant liberties with history—but may include the kind of language that indicates that it is not based on historic fact. That is, the studio may hint that the events could have happened. We do not know that they did, and we do not know that they did not.

Is the reviewer, then, expected to become an historian to check the accuracy of film fact? No, that is not likely, given the number of films produced and the demands on his time. The critic, with not only the luxury of time but also the responsibility of evaluating, not just reviewing, is much more likely to also be historian, and can deal with this. Both writers learn to read between the lines of publicity releases, and eventually become skilled at saying what was, and what might have been. The underlying argument is whether the historical inaccuracy added to or detracted from the overall effect.

Some years ago, during the early days of contact lenses, an actor named Chuck Connors (star of TV's "The Rifleman") was chosen to play the lead in a movie about the Indian Geronimo. The actor's eyes were bright blue, and it turned out he could not wear contacts. Not to worry. The studio dug into its Indian fact file and determined that there were indeed, on occasion, blue-eyed Indians. So although no one said the chief had blue eyes, the studio pointed out that he could have had them. Or if not him, another chief. In this instance the movie itself was a bomb, and no one knows how much of a factor the blue eyes were.

Developing an Eye for the Obvious

How does the reviewer check on the accuracy of costumes, dialogue, makeup, and hairstyles? He can't, unless he happens to have done a great deal of reading about a certain historical period. But he can develop a sharp enough eye to pick out the obvious. Film insiders have story after story of slip-ups, such as sports cars in the distance of Renaissance dramas, wrist watches on 18th century pirates, and clean cheeks on virile men just returned from months in the wilderness. Beards do not grow in low-budget films.

These small items should be part of the review only if they add considerably or detract considerably from the film.

Sound Tracks

Most contemporary films come with a sound track. The music, unless the film is a musical, is designed to support and to enhance the action. Some indication of the importance the studio places on the music can be found in the placement in the credits of composer and conductor, as well as in the advance material the film produces. The reviewer will find it difficult to pay too much attention to the music without spending less time evaluating the action before him. If it is particularly inappropriate, that should be brought out, just as if it is particularly memorable, that too should be mentioned.

One of the important factors in the success of "The Big Chill" was the background music, which not only dated the action, but also served as a constant reminder of the critical years when the actors first knew each other. Much of the success of "Tender Mercies" was due to the authenticity of the music. In this highly successful film Robert Duvall not only studied with established country-western stars, but did his own guitar playing and singing.

In films such as these, the reviewer attempts to find out who composed the music and what films he has written for before. If the normal releases do not include this information, which would be surprising, a quick call to the studio will. Then, without losing sight of the action on screen, the reviewer will determine if the music is a significant or an incidental factor. Of course when sound track albums are being hawked in the lobby, or when a song from the film is on all the Top 40 radio stations, we have what could be called a *valuable clue*. A popular song that "makes the charts" not only brings in revenue for the record company and the film studio, but also serves as a constant reminder that the film is playing nearby. A hit song can be excellent publicity.

Special Effects

In recent years, notably since the late 1970s, special effects have become an important part of many films, particularly adventure stories. Surely Hollywood has come a long way since the days of the glorious "Gone With The Wind," when the back lot of a major studio was set on fire to simulate the burning of Atlanta and, obviously, there was only time—and fuel—for one take. But today's craftsmen and camera technicians, working with scale models and optical effects, can make virtually anything appear on screen.

HOLLYWOOD DOES NOT MAKE BAD FILMS

Most of what has been discussed so far will add to the writer's understanding of, and explanation of, the film, and why it is or is not worth the viewer's trouble. But there is more. Nobody connected with the film industry will admit that there is such a thing as a bad film, at least not publicly. In the film business there are great films, good films, less good films, and films that represent interesting or unique ideas or interpretations. There are no bad films, only some less succesful efforts that for some reason failed to reach their potential. Yet, obviously not all efforts are worth the price of admission. The reviewer learns to read between the lines as a film is in production and nearing release to get some early idea of how good, or less good, it will turn out to be.

Accuracy

Now the reviewer deals with film accuracy, which can be a problem. How does he really know what people say when they are being knifed? When they realize that they have ingested poison? When they discover gold? What actually is the procedure in a court of law? Here the writer is on more familiar ground. If he has come up through the ranks of general assignment reporter he has, most likely, covered a trial, as well as worked with the police. If he has studied life in the raw through his newspaper work, he is better prepared to comment on life as portrayed on the screen.

But to determine the accuracy of dialect, foreign languages, and cultures, to say nothing of obscure historical events or facts, is another matter. In these instances the writer leans on two terms familiar to all entertainment writers, *believability* and *credibility*.

Believability. Believability refers to acting. Do the reviewer and the audience really believe that that actor up there is in love with that woman? Is that soldier up there really ready to give up his life for a buddy? Would anybody in his right mind believe that sad story the blonde is giving out? If the writer can believe it, it is believable. If he can't, it isn't.

The photography might be exciting, the music great, the actors attractive, but if you cannot believe they are really who they are pretending to be, the movie is in trouble.

Credibility. Credibility refers to events, to things. Could an actor fall 100 feet and land on a mattress and walk away? Could a soldier, shot through the chest, run 100 yards and throw a war-winning hand grenade another 100 before falling to the ground? Could that masked man, while riding full speed on his horse, really shoot the gun out of the hand of the bad guy? Could those men really have been on that desert island for two months without growing beards?

That is credibility, or the lack of it. This is not to suggest that all reviewers, or all audiences, for that matter, are alike. They differ widely in what they look for and what they expect on the screen. But these differences will be in terms of what is credible, what is believable, not in the importance of judging credibility and believability.

Pace, Climax, and Resolution. There are then the matters of pace, climax, and resolution. Pace refers to the speed (or lack of it) with which things take place, and is the responsibility of the director and the film editor. The director's role is generally understood; not so the editor's. The director sets out to tell a story. His skill and experience tell him how to create a certain mood for a certain scene, and when he has finished his task there may be enough film exposed for several movies. Now the editor comes in and snips and cuts and pastes, turning the raw product into a finished movie. Directors leave cameras running well after the scene is over; editors remove the unneeded film and see that the film runs smoothly. Some directors take a keen interest in editing, and lean over the editor's shoulder as he works. Others finish an assignment and move quickly on to another, not being concerned about what the editor does to the film. Still others do the rough editing themselves before turning the film over to the film editor. In any event, these two are most responsible for pace.

Skilled directors of comedy anticipate laugh lines, yet do not leave seconds-long pauses for the laugh. Rather, they will create "business" or add dialogue in the form of throwaway lines to cover the action during laughter. They take into account both possibilities: The audience will laugh, or it won't. If it does, nothing vital has been covered up. If it does not, there is no awkward pause on screen while nothing happens. Poor direction or editing that leaves painful pauses while the audience does not laugh destroys pace. Pace is one of those factors that is most effective when unnoticed.

The same reasoning pertains to resolution and climax. When something that appears early in the film is not resolved—when there are questions at the conclusion about a certain person or event—there are two probable reasons: carelessness or budget. Either the producers were anxious to get the film out in general release, and sent it out without double checking for any loose ends, or they ran out of money and there was none left for refilming. Such oversights should be mentioned. These things occur because most directors do not feel they are bound to the letter of the script, and will improvise during filming if it seems appropriate. Few films come out of the editor's room exactly as the script, which was completed months earlier, indicated. Every film risks the possibility that in-production changes left some things unresolved.

The climax comes at the end of the film, unless there are matters to be resolved after the climax, in which case it comes near the end. When the climax is properly placed, the film has a logical conclusion, and the audience is satisfied. If the climax is too early the natives get restless. A properly placed climax gives the film a feeling of completeness; everything came about satisfactorily. This does not mean the film was successful as a whole, just that it made sense. Every film should be planned around a series of high and low points, depending on the goals of the writer, director, or producer. When things go well and the direction is smooth and the audience is left happy and satisfied, then pace, resolution, and climax have been dealt with well. The credit goes to the director.

Clarity. Clarity is not as important, perhaps, as pace, resolution, and climax, but a possible angle upon which to build a review. It should be reasonably obvious to the average viewer what is going on on the screen. The timid producer–director makes things too clear, overexplaining the obvious, and his or her film becomes a bore. The egocentric filmmaker feels it is the responsibility of the audience to discover his or her message, and his or her film is a puzzle.

The great Italian director Federico Fellini made puzzling, intriguing films. When reporters asked what the films meant, the maestro said "I don't know. I wait until you review them and tell me." The best films fall into a happy middle ground, expressed by the Ideal Audience: "Make me think, please, but not too much."

Here Comes the PR

Another aspect affecting the review is hype, or PR, or advance paper, or promos. In spite of the fact that the critic usually ignores this aspect of the business, and even though the reviewer would like to, he cannot and he should not. It is, simply, there. It is not unusual for a film to be budgeted at $12 million with the expectation that an additional 50% will be spent on promotion. With some films, the promotional budget reaches or even exceeds the cost of actual filming.

The alert writer wonders why. This information reaches him through the studio itself, in the form of releases; or over the wires of the major news services; or through comments by New York and Hollywood gossip columnists; or telephone tips from friendly agents; or even from such sources as business and professional publications.

Perhaps the producers feel they have a genuine smash hit on their hands, and each promotional dollar will be doubled or even tripled at the box office. There may be a currency to the film that prompts the producer to seek the largest possible immediate audience. When Sandra Day O'Connor was appointed to the United States Supreme Court, the promotional budget of a film with a similar theme went up. However, the current practice seems to be to capitalize on current events by rushing "made for television" movies onto the tube. History has shown so far that such efforts, although they may draw modest ratings, are not quality offerings, because their production schedules are only a fraction of those assigned to normal theater films.

Many big-budget films turn out to be terrible, and the producers feel they have to pump money into promotion to recover even a part of their investment. After all, the public is so used to hype that a film with none, and no critical acclaim, will die unseen and unmourned.

Nevertheless, the newspaper should run promotional stories—feature articles and pictures on actors and directors and events surrounding the filming of a story—even though it may bomb at the box office. No one can be absolutely sure the film will fail, and the industry should be given the right to make its own mistakes, rather than expect to be saved by the nation's press. Finally, the public has a legitimate interest in the box office flops as well as the hits.

If every film that came to town was an Academy Award winner the public would quickly get sated on quality. There needs to be some basis for comparison. The intelligent and conscientious entertainment editor will not go overboard in terms of space and stories and pictures about what he feels is not a good film, but neither will he completely ignore it. There is bound to be someone who likes the film, regardless of what the experts say. There is a theater in California doing a brisk business showing films on everybody's "all-time worst" list. These "so bad they're good" movies are doing as well as their more honored brethren down the street.

Here is an example of a highly touted film that fell considerably short of its promise. The Boulder, Colorado *Daily Camera's* Kathryn Bernheimer gave it fair treatment:[1]

POLICE ACADEMY

By Kathryn Bernheimer
Camera Film and Theater Critic

"Police Academy" is part "Porky's," part "Animal House"—a movie as piggy as they come.

The premise of this anarchic comedy is that a liberal (and therefore apparently mis-

---

[1]Courtesy of the Boulder, CO *Daily Camera*, March 23, 1984.

guided) lady mayor has decided to make the entry requirements to the police academy less strict in order to avoid discrimination.

The result is a lot of fat, stupid, violent, clumsy, shy or otherwise unsuitable recruits frolicking and fumbling through training together. The word is out that anybody can become a policeman or policewoman, and every misfit in town signs up for reasons unknown. Something to do with dignity.

There's the pampered socialite (Kim Cattrall), a gentle but not too jolly black giant (Bubba Smith), a Latin lover more interested in sex than violence (Andrew Rubin), an accident-prone milquetoast (Bruce Mahler), a one-man army whose gung is always ho (David Graf), and a woman whose voice never rises above a stuttering whisper (Marion Ramsey).

Then there's our reluctant hero, a young man who gets into a little harmless trouble and is faced with the choice of going to jail or finishing the training program.

Steve Guttenberg plays Carey Mahoney, the hapless schmuck who slowly learns that happiness is a warm gun. His sidekick (Michael Winslow), whose ability to create sound effects is the best running gag in the movie, unfortunately serves no other purpose.

"Police Academy" starts off as a slap-happy, slap-dash movie, a raunchy and rowdy affair filled with the staples of mindless comedy. When the raw recruits get guns, however, the movie is no longer just harmless fun. In fact, it inadvertently starts to get a little scary.

The movie falls apart in the last half hour, when a riot breaks out and the recruits are called into action. The attempt to move from comedy to action/adventure just doesn't work. Do the filmmakers really expect us to respect the characters whose incompetence we've been laughing at?

There are a few laughs in this story of mean sergeants, silly student pranks and randy antics, but ultimately "an action-comedy that chronicles the conversion of this year's kooks into next year's cops" isn't a very funny idea.

This reviewer categorized the film immediately by comparing it to "Porky's" and "Animal House," two earlier releases that achieved some popular, although practically no critical, acclaim. Formula movies like this do not take much direction, which is why that aspect is all but overlooked. One reason the summary dominates the review is that the accompanying promotions on television and in the press suggested fun and excitement that are not really in the movie.

To consider another intangible, it is not difficult to estimate how long it will take for a major motion picture to be filmed, edited, and released. In fact, when the announcement of a new film comes through the trade press and thereby to the newspaper, it usually includes a projection of how long a shooting schedule is planned. If this period passes and the picture is not in release, and several more months go by and there is still no sign of it, something is up.

The indications are that unless there is some particularly improper content, the film is not very good and it will be either held for release later, the name will be changed, it will be sold to television, or given over to international (but not domestic) release. The reviewer can usually figure this out, and the answer will tell him even more about the film than the amount of publicity material that has been piling up on his desk. One reason for delaying the release of a film is that although it might not be bad, it simply does not equal the hyperbole attached to it during filming, and rather than anger an audience the producer will simply keep it on the shelf.

Other Aspects and Intangibles

Other factors that may or may not become part of the review are color, length, intermissions, and casting. A late 1980s trend has been to credit the casting director—the person who fills the stage with extras, as well as principles and supporting actors—soon after the title. The producer is ultimately responsible for outdoor scenes because these are often a function of budget, and this includes realistic or unrealistic treatment of weather, and the topicality of dress, cars, and language.

The final intangible is the one that is never expected. The highly successful film "The Sting" had one major flaw, or it would have been a flaw if the producers had not had enough sense to announce it in advance. This Paul Newman–Robert Redford favorite re-introduced America to the magical music of the ragtime composer Scott Joplin. Yet the time of "The Sting" was the 1930s, and Joplin's music represented the turn of the century. The music of the 1930s was boogie woogie and jazz, not ragtime. But the producers felt the quaint and nostalgic strains of Joplin were better suited for audiences of the 1970s, so they used them. But they made no pretense that the music fit the period. The music fit the mood, and their purposes, so it was used.

Chapter Five
Television—The Awesome Medium

RADIO'S CONTRIBUTION

People in the entertainment world have always used the term *Radio–TV*, rather than separating the activities into two categories, and that is the term that normally appears in a listing of the arts. In the early days of radio, legitimate drama and music were plentiful. As late as the 1950s station WBBM in Chicago employed enough musicians so that everything musical that came over the air was live. It was probably the last station in America to give up and go to recorded music.

These musical and dramatic shows were frequently reviewed, much as music and theater are today. But there was far more on radio to attract listeners. Just about everything that has ever appeared on television had its beginnings on radio—soap operas, medical shows, quiz shows, police and detective and cowboy shows—even "Candid Camera" began on radio as "Candid Mike." Radio programs attracted huge audiences, comparable to television today, and a host of stars—Jack Benny, Fred Allen, Arthur Godfrey, Red Skelton, and later Dean Martin and Jerry Lewis first earned national attention through the airwaves. Hardly had radio become a viable commercial medium than sporting events began to take up air time.

Yet, there has been nothing on radio to attract the critic or reviewer for years, as television and changing audiences have resulted in a new type of radio programming. Occasionally some old radio shows will be revived—not recreated, with new casts, but old transcriptions will be played—such as "The Shadow," "The Green Hornet," or "The Lone Ranger." If these draw any interest from the daily press it is likely to be from the feature side. Newspapers may publish routine announcements about them, but even such one-time classics seldom draw reviews.

Richard Foreman of Stamford, Connecticut, heads his own radio consultant service, Richard A. Foreman Associates, and has worked with major networks as well as smaller radio chains and individual stations. He makes a good living by understanding radio audiences, and as he travels across the country he pays attention to what the press has to say about radio programming. He has been involved with this aspect of broadcasting for more than 15 years, and cannot remember the last time he saw a review of a radio program. What's more, he sees no return to radio drama or the kind of musical or documentary programs that once regularly drew critical comment from the print media (personal communication, May, 1983). Radio only makes the news now as a news story, such as a station changing ownership, format, or call letters. There are stories in newspapers in many larger markets about ratings and personnel changes, but these have nothing to do with individual program content.

THE IMPACT OF TELEVISION

Television, the infant among the arts and the media, changes too quickly for anyone to be able to make pronouncements about it that will stand the test of time. By the mid-1980s it seemed to have gone the way of radio as far as earning critical attention in most of the nation's press. Reviews of television programs as such had practically disappeared, replaced by previews and interviews. This was a paradox, because the medium remains the most popular, the most awesome, and the most limited of our arts. One reason might be that a television program, a single broadcast, is impervious to a review. Even a series can generally ignore critical comment. Unlike films, books, theater, and dance, and to a degree art and music, negative comments mean nothing to TV. Reviewers and critics alike feel a responsibility to keep an eye on the product and alert audiences to shabby material. But by the time a program reaches television, all the decisions have been made, all the funding secured.

Consider the incredible impact of television. In 1956 actress Mary Martin recreated her Broadway role as "Peter Pan" in a live television production. It was widely publicized and highly successful. Sociologists noted that for the first time in our recorded history, with the exception of sleeping, a majority of Americans were doing the same thing at the same time. More than half of us were watching the tube. In the following decade, technological improvements allowed more than 200 million Americans to watch all or parts of that grim weekend when a young President was shot, his assailant slain on live television, and an unforgettable cortege wound its doleful way through the streets of Washington, DC.

Later, Olivier's epic film "Hamlet" was shown on television. Just as in its first existence it reached more viewers within 6 months than had seen a live presentation in the preceding 4 centuries, so did one exposure on TV reach as many as had seen the great film in theaters.

Television dwarfs the other arts. A book sells 100,000 copies and is declared a best-seller; a Broadway play enjoys a 200-day run, is seen by as many as 100,000 people, and becomes a smash hit; a touring exhibit of the treasures of King Tut's tomb attracts several million viewers in six major cities. In the 1980s a television show that could not attract 10 times that number was a flop. Only best-attended films came close to television in terms of audience, and a film must build up its numbers over a period of time.

THE MEDIUM'S BUILT-IN DRAWBACKS

From a purely critical standpoint, American commercial television has several major drawbacks.

Problems with Commercials

The first is that television programs must be written to allow for frequent interruptions. Even though on first-run major network offerings there can be almost 30 minutes before the first commercial message, they then come with ever-increasing frequency. Nevertheless, they pay the bills, and when there is indeed something artistic and worthwhile on television it was put there by the people who sell us aspirin and beer, for example.

Problems with Time

A second drawback is that there are a predetermined number of minutes and seconds into which action must fit. On the stage, the skilled actor is trained to be flexible. If he is going over well with an enthusiastic audience he may add seconds to a scene, drawing all the drama or poignancy from it that he can. (Or if he is falling on his face he can speed up the action and end the agony sooner.) On TV there is no such luxury. A second spent in one scene must be recouped before the next commercial. There are 30-minute programs (which allow only around 24 minutes of noncommercial time), 60-minute programs, occasional 90-minute and 2-hour treatments, and even mini-series that extend over several days. These give the writer more leeway, because time can be filled by excerpts from the previous program and previews of upcoming ones. But there can hardly be uninterrupted entertainment when there are continual reminders of what has already been seen, and what will be seen next. The recent decision of the Federal Communications Commission (FCC) to remove limitations on the amount of commercial time that could be sold gave a little leeway, but not much.

Appetite of the Medium

A third problem is the appetite of the medium. An entire season of Broadway openings would last little more than a month on television. The product of every domestic motion picture company would not fill a season on one network. Day after day, night after night, television demands input. The advertisers, enriched by the audiences that television attracts, stand by with fists full of dollars. Consider the talent necessary to produce new versions of three to six programs a night for each major network; words pour out of typewriters onto scripts and come babbling out of the TV set at an astonishing rate. Everything is rushed.

In a successful 60-minute weekly series the cast is expected to produce as many as 26 episodes each year. Allowing for no hiatus, this gives them 2 weeks for each installment. Yet, many episodes in a series of this type have as much dialogue for leading players as a full-length movie. But, in film, the cast has at least 2 months, sometimes 6, sometimes 12 months, to produce a quality product. What can television possibly produce in a tenth of that time?

Faced with these problems, the typical viewer turns to the videocassette store. Television simply does not hold the promise it did years ago. What would the early pioneers have thought of a television channel that is nothing more than a visual catalogue shopping activity? Yet, such have been the demands for entertainment material that shopping by video can be more profitable to the local station owner than showing reruns from the golden age of television.

Worthwhile material can be found on television, although it seems easier to deplore the lack of quality on the little screen than to applaud something good. When the writer does get the chance to comment on something original and particularly well done he should apply the same standards he would use in evaluating film or theater, keeping in mind the limitations of the medium. When something truly golden comes along, the fact that these obstacles have been overcome makes it really remarkable.

By the mid-1980s, television had settled into a pattern where only a small percentage of what was seen called for any kind of actual artistic creativity, and much of that was on public television, which seemed overburdened with programs from England. Yet the stations would point out that there was nothing comparable coming from American producers. True, many public stations would commission interesting and at times excellent documentaries, but little in the way of original drama or music.

And on the commercial side, many hours were filled with sports, and more by game and talk shows. Still more were taken up by movies, and it is not fair to be critical of theatrical films shown on television. The film was made to be seen at one sitting with no interruptions. The artistic intent is changed by the insertion of commercials, to say nothing of editing that may be necessary to make the film suitable for a home audience. Movies on commercial television should be announced, not reviewed. Finally, news programs were taking up an increasing amount of television time.

FOUR TYPES OF TV OFFERINGS

Although history indicates it is difficult to predict the future of television as an entertainment medium, there seem to be four broad categories of video activity to interest the critic and reviewer—cable, the made-for-TV movie, the special, and the start of a new season.

Cable

No one knows quite what to make of cable. It has shown some of its early promise in bringing uninterrupted material to the home viewer, for which he or she pays a monthly price, yet it has neither swept the country nor died in infancy. It is still an unknown quantity. Some, in the early days, saw it as a means of public access, not only in terms of politics and government—broadcasting city council and school board meetings—but also in terms of allowing the less talented and less wealthy to get on the air with their entertainment offerings. Some envisioned the day when every high school play, every college spring concert, every church's Messiah could be on cable television. So far this has not happened, and the industry shows no signs of going in that direction.

Most of the material on cable is sporting events, theatrical movies of recent release, or specials filmed specifically for cable. Sporting events do not require criticism, theatrical films have already been criticized in the press, and the specials are more like night club revues than anything else. They attract more and more space in the daily press in the form of advance stories, but still no regular critical comment has been forthcoming.

Made-for-TV Movies

The made-for-TV movie is similar to its theatrical counterpart with two exceptions; it is written with commercial interruptions in mind, and it must fit its time slot. The writer needs to consider both factors in his evaluation. Often, a TV film gives the feeling of being too short, or too long. Many critics have referred to this type of offering as a 30- or 60-minute program trying to masquerade as a feature-length film. They feel that the small screen must have continuous action because of the many distractions going on in the home, compared to the relative quiet of a theater. There is no flexibility in a made-for-TV movie to add seconds, even minutes, to the total running time with dramatic or extended pauses. Obviously, the trick is to find a good 1- or 2-hour idea that lends itself to commercial breaks.

When a made-for-TV movie does fit easily into its time slot, and the commercials do not destroy the line of action, the result can be memorable. This is the power of TV. Some truly remarkable stories have been presented, many dealing with vital current subjects such as rape, prison reform, AIDS, and drug abuse. The highly acclaimed docu-drama ''Adam'' was the catalyst for a renewed national interest in locating missing children. There have been other powerful messages, artistic and creative in the truest sense. Here, both critic and reviewer frequently break a normal rule, which is not to mention the sponsors. When the people who put up the money have the sensitivity and intelligence to allow excellent treatment of a difficult subject, and even tone down their own messages, they deserve praise. Of course, there is always a grain of salt with these matters. The generous sponsor who allows a program to be aired with virtually no interruptions for his messages may spend many dollars in other media proclaiming his own generosity in not diluting the television program with unnecessary messages.

The Special

The next category of television fare is the *special*, a broad term overused by the industry. Television producers are most likely to use cost as a factor in determining what is a special, rather than quality, but this can easily backfire, as the viewing audience has come to expect more from a special than from an ordinary program. At first, a special represented a major effort, a musical, dramatic, or comedy event that was indeed a highlight of the season. No more. Now anything that is not regular programming can be a special.

Entertainment specials can employ drama, music, and combinations of these, including dance, magic, circus performances, even vaudeville. They involve talented performers, they are carefully rehearsed, and there is creativity that can be appreciated. If the program is to be reviewed, the presence or absence of talent, creativity, and the overall production can be the basis for the commentary. Many American families build their evenings, if not their weeks, around what specials are to be aired. (There is, however, a new element in this habit that may affect this analysis; that is the large number of families who tape one program while watching another, then watch the taped one later. The problem is up to the rating services to determine not only how many people are watching, but also how many are taping.) The networks usually provide advance screenings of specials for local television writers, so that local previews can appear

Criticism after the fact seems to be a lost art, gone with the golden days of live television drama. But quality television drama should still be reviewed. It is not a matter of recording the event for posterity, because so much material comes across on television, or because the program may be repeated at a later date. Rather, the review should be written as recognition of the creative effort that went into the program. Critics and reviewers alike may be all but voiceless when evaluating new programs and schedules, but they can add opinion as a valuable postscript, and with luck have some effect on future offerings.

Normally, the preview written by a television writer appears the day of the program, and given the amount of publicity the program has probably had it is unlikely that many viewers, anticipating the entertainment delight promised by hundreds of thousands of dollars of promotion, will change their minds on the basis of one dissenting voice lost in the jungle of paid ads.

Modern technology, however, offers some hope in this area. Television programs are now measured for audience size at the beginning, during, and near the end. Formerly a highly touted special might start off with a high rating, perhaps a 40% share of the audience. Advertisers were delighted. But newer, more accurate rating methods can show that at the beginning of the second hour the audience may have decreased considerably, and all but disappeared by the end. This means that the television preview may become a more powerful voice in assuring television quality in that no longer will a weak program be able to get by on the basis of previewing hyperbole. That would be nice.

The Start of a New Season

The category of new programs, which come during those times when networks reveal their new season's offerings, offers more fruitful ground for the writer who hopes to have some effect on the quality of television. It used to happen all at once; there was a general agreement as to when the fall season began, and the viewer was faced daily with choices of which new program to see. The good thing about that was that it took the average viewer at least 3 weeks to sample all the new network offerings, and those responsible for taking programs off the air or allowing them to stay were tolerant, and usually gave the programs 8 or 10 weeks to make some impact. Now it is a different, much more competitive business. The networks reveal their new schedules at different times, and while one is displaying its new wares, the others are trying to damage their rival's audience by showing reruns of specials, first-run movies, or other tried and true programs. Television programs now must win an early audience to have any hope of success. Any show that does not attract a significant number of viewers within 5 or 6 weeks is not long for the airwaves. Critics and viewers alike had to beg NBC to keep "Hill Street Blues" and "St. Elsewhere" on the air in the face of disappointing early ratings. In the old days, most programs had a full season, 39 weeks, as a normal life expectancy, and only the very, very poor shows were taken off earlier.

AGAIN THE STRONG BEGINNING

The television review begins with a strong opening statement. Basic identification includes the network and usually the local channel. Current practice seems to be not to use call letters. If the sponsor's contribution is noteworthy it should certainly be part of the review, although the sponsor should not automatically be mentioned.

An important part of identification is a description of the type of program in terms of time. The effort is more likely to be 1 hour, or 2 hours, or several hours over a period of days or weeks. The current practice also seems to be to identify actors in terms of other television roles. When comic Don Knotts appears on a television game show he is referred to as " 'Three's Company's' Don Knotts." Daniel J. Travanti stepped out of his award-winning "Hill Street Blues" role to star in

"Adam," and advance stories and reviews alike called him " 'Hill Street's' Daniel J. Travanti."

Leading actors on some hour-long series have more dialogue than stars of full-length feature films. They talk, the film stars act, because there is not enough time in the TV business to do more than become familiar with the lines. This can make the reviewer's task difficult as he tries to assess such factors as accent, believability, writing, or motivation. Camera work is usually simpler on television, because directors will not risk artistic shots and angles for an easily distracted audience more attuned to 30-minute situation comedies. Successful television dramas are those that can survive the viewer missing brief parts of the program.

Opinion includes the same factors that are pertinent to any of the performing arts, although less emphasis seems to be placed on believability and credibility.

Summary in the television review varies from that found in drama and film criticism in that most television performers are associated with other activities, usually other television roles or appearances. In film and drama that is not always a factor. There seems to be a general recognition by the press that the short rehearsal and production time associated with television means that an actor appears far more often on the small than on the large screen. Add to this the reruns that are the staple of independent stations, and the chances are that a familiar television face is familiar as a result of many, rather than a few, appearances.

Public television would seem to offer the entertainment writer his only real chance to be critical with his medium, but public television has fallen on hard times, and the money to produce quality drama is simply not there any more. There is currently talk about public stations running commercials; an experiment involving 12 public stations was conducted in 1984, and more such tests are expected to follow. Cynics say there are commercial messages already in the form of listings of donors who made the program possible; certainly there has been a change from the early practice of simply identifying a sponsor to now including at least a brief corporate slogan or indication of product or service. And what used to be a few words has grown into a sentence, even two, as corporate modesty seems to have taken a back seat to the realities of advertising.

What quality there is is likely to be imported from England, and, although public television is so far unencumbered by commercials, it still must fit into predictable time periods, or the program must be fleshed out by a panel of experts discussing what has just been seen. This fare might be attractive to theater buffs, but is deadly dull to most of the rest of the home audience. Imported fare may be good, but leaves blocks of time to be filled; and locally produced drama will be squeezed into the same old 30- or 60-minute or 2-hour time blocks.

Chapter Six
Music—The Divided Art

Classical and modern drama, comedy, and tragedy, are all the province of the theater writer. Modern, traditional, and representational art, even sculpture, often are one writer's bailiwick. A book reviewer critiques prose and poetry, fiction and nonfiction.

But that is not the way it works with music.

DIVISION AND SUBDIVISION

Music is the medium of endless variety. As a subject for criticism it is not only divided, but subdivided, and comes with a clear distinction between the old and the new, to say nothing of the many further divisions within each camp.

On the large, well-staffed newspaper the classical music writers deal with orchestral, ensemble, solo, and vocal performances, and if the staff is large, one writer may concentrate on opera. A specialist in dance is often counted among the music writers.

Across the room one or more people deal with popular music, a broad category that includes rock, jazz, blues, soul, big band, country-western, and blue grass, as well as variations on these. The popular music writer must also be versatile.

It is interesting to note that nowhere else in the newspaper is there such a clear-cut division. In the sports department all writers cover all sports, and often change beats. Political writers cover both parties, and report on state, local, and national politics. It is only on the smaller or understaffed newspapers that an entertainment writer doubles in classic and popular music.

The distance between the extremes in music, between a punk rock concert where the performers (and audience) wear outlandish costumes, dye their hair green, and throw themselves wildly about the stage, and a distinguished string quartet playing an evening of Haydn, is considerable.

CLASSICAL IS TRADITIONAL

Classical music is written in certain traditional forms, normally for an audience, but not for a 4,000-seat concert hall. Much classical music was commissioned, written for a formal grouping of musicians and an indefinite number of listeners or celebrants.

Classical music calls for traditional instruments—even the 100-year-old saxaphone is still considered too modern for purists—a minimum of improvisation, and a great deal of interpretation.

It has been extant for hundreds of years, but contemporary composers write what is still correctly called *classical music* in that their output satisfies basic conditions of form and performance. Classical compositions tend to be more difficult to perform, and require more rehearsal time, preparation, and technical skill than popular music.

Reviewers covering noteworthy classical music can certainly do more than simply report. In the following example, *Sacramento Bee* writer Robert Masullo covers a performance by the San Francisco Opera, a widely acclaimed group, assisted by notable artists from abroad. This is the kind of assignment where, unless something drastic goes wrong, it is a foregone conclusion that the evening will be successful. The work has survived for a century, the individual artists have impressive credentials, and the opera company is well established. This is how Masullo handled it:[1]

'DUCHESSE' IS A DELIGHTFUL TREAT

By Robert A. Masullo
Bee Reviewer

SAN FRANCISCO—French pastry, no matter how fine the ingredients, should be consumed only in small quantities. Otherwise the sweetness may become overwhelming. The delectable confection, "La Grande Duchesse de Gerolstein," from the Offenbach bakery, performed Sunday for the first time ever in a regular season by the San Francisco Opera, may be the prime example.

This mega-caloric treat as delivered couldn't have been more delightful. Provided, of course, this sort of work doesn't become too frequent and leave inadequate room for the more substantial fare of Verdi, Wagner and friends, it should be applauded. And Sunday it was—loud and long.

Many elements go into this. Brilliantly designed by Hubert Monloup and staged by Maurice Ducasse, both in American debuts, the presentation visually resembled

---

[1]Courtesy of the Sacramento *Bee*, November 8, 1983.

a party cake of elaborate detail. Choreography, by Marika Sakellariou, especially the can-can-like number between Scene 1 and 2 of the final (third) act, is remarkably ef-fervescent. Thomas J. Munn's lighting effects, especially the half-tone greens and blues suggesting greed and envy, are similarly palate pleasers. And Marc Soustrot's con-ducting is properly spirited.

The sweets themselves, however, are super performances by three singing actors who seem born for their parts—Tibere Raffalli, a Corsican tenor as Fritz, the apple of the duchess' eye; Michel Trempont, a Belgian buffa-baritone as the pompous Gen. Boum, and, especially, Regine Crespin as the duchess, the bed-room-eyed commander-in-chief of Gerolstein, the imaginary German city-state.

Crespin, a big hit last season in San Francisco in "The Dialogue of the Carma-lites," has built a substantial part of her substantial reputation—she may be the most popular soprano in France—with the duchess role. And it is easy to see why. Both her singing and acting seem to perfectly capture the qualities of a wealthy, powerful, middle-aged plus woman with a weakness for young men. Her voice in mid-range is as rich as the personage she represents. Her insertion of occasional English words in the French (e.g., "Not bad, huh?" Or the operetta's moral, "If you can't have what you love, love what you have.") adds markedly to the humor.

Raffalli, making his American debut, has almost feminine good looks. Merging them with a sly manner and first-rate singing—reminiscent of the young Mario Del Monaco—Raffalli comes off as a most believable Fritz. One can easily see why the duchess promotes him from private to general.

Trempont, also on a U.S. stage for the first time, struts and scowls and booms through his lines as Gen. Boum in an hilarious fashion. His voice, resonating with the proper bluster, is always captivating.

Add to these fine performances by the beautiful Kaaren Erickson, as Fritz's true love, Wanda; the handsome baritone John Matthews as Baron Puck, and tenor Remy Corazza as Prince Paul, whom the duchess reluctantly settles for. And skilled work by those in minor roles and from the choruses.

The spirited work by Jakob Eberst—as Jacques Offenbach was known before mov-ing from Cologne to Paris—is performed in the War Memorial Opera House in a hap-py, snappy, charming fashion. Seeing it could make any day a holiday.

This reviewer chose to deal with the overall effects of the program, rather than concentrate on the singers. Equally important, he educates as well as reviews, pointing out that the popular Offenbach had changed his name as his fortunes improved.

The writer reviewing an old favorite—known as a "war horse" in the business—knows his readers will be familiar with it. Such is not the case, however, when the performance is modern. William Glackin, also of the *Bee*, traveled to San Francis-co for quite a different event, a program featuring modernist John Cage, and the review had to include much more explanation than Masullo's coverage of Offen-bach. Here the review seems to be mainly a feature story, with comment on the actual performance secondary.[2]

---

[2]Courtesy of the Sacramento *Bee*, November 28, 1983.

CAGE: HE'S A MASTER OF COMPOSITION

By William Glackin
Bee Reviewer

SAN FRANCISCO—If John Cage did not exist, it would be necessary to invent him. For nearly a half century he has been jarring our conventionalities, needling our imaginations, showing us new ways to view the art and the world. Quite aside from his compositions, he has become, at 71, his own best masterpiece.

Cage himself would probably resist such pronouncements. Certainly he did not look historic Friday night at 7:30 as he ambled onto the stage in Davies Symphony Hall to begin an evening in his honor on the New and Unusual Music Series of the San Francisco Symphony. His denim jeans and jacket were faded, his smile amiable, his manner unassuming. He looked around the hall in a manner prophetic of a remark he was presently to make in his lecture: "I welcome whatever happens next." The audience did not wake up to his presence until he was center stage; then a long wave of applause rolled through the big hall.

As a prelude to the concert, he sat at a table and read one of his famously provocative and sometimes mysterious lectures. He once explained, "I don't give these lectures out of a need to surprise people, but out of a need for poetry." The same might be said for the surprising poetry of his music.

These remarks, delivered in a light, gentle tone, were called "Composition in Retrospect," and had been given originally to a workshop of young composers in England in 1981. "The music is there before it is written," he told them. "Composition is only the means of finding out that that is the case."

"Music never stops," he said. "It is we who turn away." That had a kind of poignance, for people have been turning away from his radical musical ideas for years, often with indignation.

For the concert, he sat on a chair against the wall at the left of the platform, following everything with evident interest. The program drew from both sides of the watershed of Cage's life, his discovery of Zen in the mid-1940s. Before that, his compositions were innovative in many startling ways but mostly followed traditional structure and methods; there was a beat, for instance. After that, he introduced elements of chance and choice into his music, a move which influenced a whole string of younger composers. With equally influential results, he also made use of silence, and the idea of duration as a substitute for definite time.

Examples of pre-Zen works were "First Construction (in Metal)," composed nearly 50 years ago, and "Credo in Us," written for a dance as a satire on life in the United States. ("When I wrote it," he said, "it was very serious. It gets funnier and funnier as the years go by.") The first employs only metal instruments, but they include several "thunder sheets," brake drums and many chiming instruments from Asia. The "Credo" introduces a radio (tuned in at random), tapes of Tchaikovsky's music, tuned coffee cans and such, and has a tremendous piano part. Both pieces were full of melody and lively with rhythms, and absolutely delightful.

The finale was "Concert for Piano and Orchestra," (1958) with Joseph Kubera as soloist and John Adams the conductor. The piece is for any number of players (about 15 here) who use not only conventional instruments but such oddities as a wine bottle, a sea shell, toy horns and a balloon (blown up and punctured). They also make surprising sounds of their own. (The trombonist barked, the tuba player screamed into the bell of his horn.) The effect is of many disconnected sounds, produced according to a mysterious plan. It seems very free and spontaneous, and does involve choice, but actually the 63 pages of music describe 84 different methods of music making for the players, and take a lot of study.

In the middle of the evening the composer read excerpts from "MUOYCE (MUS-IC JOYCE)" (1983), a collection of phrases, words, syllables and letters selected by chance methods from James Joyce's final masterpiece, "Finnegan's Wake." For 12 minutes, the audience sat in absolute attention while Cage chanted the largely unintelligible text. Partly because it sounded like Gregorian chant, the scene was like a rite. It would appear that John Cage has become something of a cult figure, too. But he is too brilliant and valuable a man to be dismissed as a mere guru.

Although the extremes of music may seem miles—or years—apart, there are instances where the lines between them all but disappear. In the Cage example, the writer felt he had to explain the composer to his readers, and the review contained a lot of explanation, because Cage is modern and not at all in the typical Beethoven–Mozart mode.

Now consider turn-of-the-century popular music, as represented by the great ragtime composers. Here is music in a transitional stage, going from popular to light classical. (In similar fashion the music of the Beatles, once scorned by parents of young fans, now pops up with regularity in concerts by the Boston Pops Orchestra.)[3]

A LONGING GLANCE AT RAGTIME

Les Zachels

Gazette Music Columnist

The pages of American musical and social history were leafed back to the turn of the century last night at the Paramount Theater.

Max Morath, America's ace ragtime piano entertainer, presented a fast-moving, two-hour concert that was truly absorbing. The Morath appearance was the final attraction of this season's Community Concert Series.

A master conversationalist, Morath has hit upon a brilliant formula that wraps his knowledge and talent at the keyboard into a neat entertainment package. His rapport with his audience is remarkable as he relates the story of the ragtime piano craze that swept the country in the first decade of the 1900s.

Morath first came to the attention of Eastern Iowans about 25 years ago when vacationing Iowans visited the popular "Melodrama" presentations at Cripple Creek, Colo.

With a refurbished Edison cylinder phonograph—the horn model—as his only stage prop, Morath launched his theme for Monday evening's program, "Living a Ragtime

---

[3]Reprinted by permission of the Cedar Rapids *Gazette*, May 3, 1983.

Life.'' His commentary covered such subjects as the early autos, women's suffrage, the double standard and social and political mores. This philosophizing was seasoned with piano rags by popular "professors" of the day, Tom Turpin, Louis Chauvez and, of course, Scott Joplin.

Particularly appealing was his glossy rendition of James Scott's "Grace and Beauty." The relating of the troubles and trials of the adventuresome "Bill Bailey" in song was an audience favorite.

Morath gave a touching tribute to Eubie Blake, who recently passed away five days after his 100th birthday. In Blake's memory, he played the "Charleston Rag," which Blake composed at age 19 but never got around to having it published until age 95.

After intermission, Morath played the number that everyone knew, the "Maple Leaf Rag" by Scott Joplin. That was the tune that served as the catalyst for the entire ragtime movement.

Morath peppered his commentary with pithy remarks. Among his best was his observation of the part played by the womenfolk of the household in the popularization of ragtime: "Mother and Grandma played the piano, Grandpa played pinochle."

Another fine presentation was his dissection of the old barnburner, "Tiger Rag." His illustration of the parts lifted from a French quadrille and a drawing room waltz was very cleverly presented. Morath quite correctly placed heavy emphasis on the role played by Scott Joplin in the composition and the popularization of this style of piano music.

Morath's playing was virtually flawless, meeting the high technical demands. His tempos were quite correctly chosen, heeding the admonition that graced all of Joplin's music, "Not to be played too fast."

For a closer, Morath accompanied himself, playing on a sound track, much to the delight of the audience.

"Living a Ragtime Life" was a first-rate commentary on the American scene.

The tone of this review seems closer to the Offenbach article then the review of John Cage. The French composer is known and accepted, the singers with the opera are established stars, and so also is the music of the American ragtime writers and the talent of Max Morath taken for granted. But Cage needs explaining.

No Fixed Number of Players

Classical orchestral music is not scored for a certain number of musicians. Composers write for strings, woodwinds, and brass, not necessarily for 40 violins, 25 assorted woodwinds, and 12 brass instruments. Most orchestra music will include parts for first and second violins, but nowhere will it say how many of each there should be.

This is often a function of the financial stability of the orchestra, and the wishes of the conductor. The conductor will know how many violins he or she wants for a Beethoven symphony for a good balance. If the violins then overpower the rest of the players, it is the conductor's fault; either there are too many of them, or the conductor is letting them play too loud.

The percussion section varies widely, depending on what is being played. It can contain 10 players or 2, although if the number is 2 they will be busy musicians. The conductor may want to add an additional 3 or 4 cellos to bring out tenor parts in some works, or will double up on flutes and oboes to enhance soprano harmonies in others. A great deal of personal interpretation is thus possible. Pianists, among the more popular soloists, come in a variety of sizes and temperaments, and bring with them, in addition to their physical ability and years of practice, certain idiosyncrasies that are theirs alone. One pianist remains calm, fingers seldom raising more than a few inches above the keyboard, back straight, shoulders even. Another, playing the same Beethoven sonata, will be all over the piano bench, arms flailing wildly overhead, chin bobbing energetically, torso bouncing from side to side, shoulders twisting in almost agonizing reaction to the music.

Which is the better? Certainly the more acrobatic gives the audience more to look at, but the question should be, which is the more musical. An experienced pianist said, "If what the player does helps him to perform, he should do it." The beginning writer needs to remember that contortions on stage are not an indication of ability, or the lack of it.

Similarly, some violin soloists bend and weave with the music, whereas others remain upright and unmoving. Conductors also come in various sizes with varying degrees of energy and mobility. Contemporary audiences may have forgotten that the term *long hair* originally applied to classical music, and came from the habit of 19th and early 20th century conductors of letting their hair grow long so that their manes could be tossed about as they lead their orchestras through Wagner and Strauss.

But it is how he or she directs, how he or she leads, how well the players follow him or her that matters. Conductors are charged with getting the most out of their musicians. Some beg, some threaten, some implore, some harangue; and some are able to get the utmost from their charges by being physical themselves. The story may indeed be apocryphal, but the great Leopold Stokowski was known to go to extremes to assure a quality performance. Before one critical concert he had difficulty getting a clarinetist to come in at exactly the right time. At the final rehearsal, Stokowski told the player that if he failed to come in on time, he would shoot him. Then on the night of the concert, just before raising his baton to begin, the legendary maestro drew a pistol from his jacket and placed it prominently on the podium, all the while glaring at the suffering clarinet player. Then he began, and the piece came off without a hitch.

Antics from the podium should be measured against results from the orchestra.

The gyrations and contortions of some currently popular musicians, although they may be original movements, are not original concepts. The great Liszt and Paganini certainly did everything they could to add drama to their virtuoso performances. The 19th century romantic masters did not have laser beam shows to enhance their performances, but Liszt was known to keep audiences waiting in absolute silence for 30 minutes before making his own grand appearance.

Help Can Be Close at Hand

The printed program notes that accompany a classical music performance can be a help, especially if used in connection with a standard reference work that provides thumbnail sketches of prominent composers. The program gives the correct spelling of names, normally the dates of the composer, and often some of the circumstances surrounding the composition itself; was it written for a royal festival for a European king, was it penned to commemorate a notable birthday, was it a product of the composer's early or late years, does it represent a certain school, or style, of composition.

The reviewer can learn about romantic, baroque, atonal, or experimental music through the program notes. He can also try to find out who writes the notes, because that person can be a valuable aide in learning to understand unfamiliar music.

The program will rarely list an encore, and they are not always announced. However it is often a well-known specialty of the performer, and the reviewer must be knowledgeable to recognize what is being played. Those writing for morning newspapers are up against a deadline and may not have time to stop backstage to get the name of the encore.

Here the writer should simply say that the performer acknowledged the audience's response with an encore. It is unprofessional (and unnecessary) to write "this reporter missed the name of the encore, but it was well received," or "deadline pressure denied the writer a chance to identify the encore." Usually an encore is a sentimental favorite or a brief and flashy showpiece. It is a way of letting the audience reward the performer, or letting the performer reward the audience. Encores deserve brief mention, nothing more.

Program notes that describe the music itself are often written by biased observers, and can be similar to overdone public relations releases. That is, they contain some truth but also a great deal of puffery. A musical composition might, as the composer hoped, suggest the crashing of waves on a distant shore, and the notes might say "One can almost hear the thunder of waves crashing on a distant shore." The writer who blithely and blindly parrots such a sentiment is not doing much of a service to his readers. No respectable reporter would passively accept a release that proclaims a certain candidate as the best qualified to serve; similarly no music writer should believe, just because the program says so, that a composition contains qualities that only the composer's immediate family could find in it.

There is a big difference in actually using a piece of equipment to produce a certain sound (cannon, airplane engines, sleigh bells) and an imaginative composer calling for a similar sound from conventional instruments (kettle drums, lower brasses, triangle).

The main objective of a classical performance is to give the music a faithful interpretation. It involves players and listeners, and the review should include audience reaction.

Preparation Before the Concert

Should the reviewer attempt to listen to a tape or recording of the music he is going to hear, and should he try to get a copy of the score so that he can follow along with the musicians? The answer is normally no on both counts. If a reviewer is able to keep in mind 2 hours of music, or if he is skilled enough to follow a complete musical score and at the same time give full attention to what he is hearing, he is far past the beginner stage. Familiarity with music helps, but the reviewer is covering a particular live performance, not a particular set of musical compositions.

Should the writer attempt to talk to the performers? Generally yes, because the more he knows about them the better able he is to understand what they are doing. This kind of interview also provides material for columns, advance stories, and anecdotes. Still, the review is not an interview story, and the writer needs to be careful not to add personal notes about the performer, but to stick to the performance. The exception would be when the interview revealed that the singer was fighting a head cold, or the pianist was recovering from a sprained wrist.

Should the writer look at other reviews based on the same musicians or the same composition? Perhaps. Beginners often do, usually with trepidation. A critical analysis of modern music by an expert could help the reviewer learn what to look for, but there is great temptation to repeat what has already been written.

The best advice for the neophyte covering classical music is to pay close attention to audience reaction, have some general idea of the purpose of the music, and not to presume knowledge he does not have. Common sense and a genuine interest make the best foundation for developing an ability to write sensibly about classical music.

THE POPULAR SIDE

Popular music is something else.

It is heard everywhere, in intimate night clubs, in large auditoriums, in gigantic stadiums, in huge, open fields. The reason for these varied venues can be given in one word: *amplification*. First megaphones, then microphones—now everything is electrified and amplified. And that is only one distinction.

Popular music compositions are usually shorter and less complicated than classical ones, allowing for a lot of improvisation and interpretation.

Popular music is a more visual experience, particularly when the performers come equipped with laser-beam light shows and innovative and outlandish costumes and behavior. When famous rock stars come to town it is not only a performance, but an event, and the reviewer is expected to do more than just comment on the music.

This is the approach Steve Morse of the *Boston Globe* took when David Bowie showed up in concert.[4]

---

[4]Reprinted courtesy of the Boston *Globe*, September 1, 1983.

BOWIE MAGIC AT ITS BEST

By Steve Morse
Globe Staff

FOXBOROUGH—Fate has smiled on David Bowie all year, and last night was no exception. No sooner did he come onstage than a drenching rainstorm miraculously stopped, enabling him to perform a show that thoroughly justified the praise he's received in one cover story after another this summer.

There were 55,000 hardy souls in attendance—5000 less than the sold-out house for the Police concert three weeks ago—and they were rewarded with a reborn Bowie who was as sleek, debonair and captivating as all the headlines have proclaimed.

The key was Bowie's conviction. He dropped his fabled masks and proved beyond a doubt he has moved from freaky chameleon to steady pro. For two hours he enchanted the crowd with music, theater, dance, mime and dramatic stage moves that encompassed bouncing and pirouetting at the mike or racing back and forth in choreographed precision with his two guitarists and two backup singers.

Dashing in white pants and suitcoat, which he later pared down to a blue shirt and suspenders, Bowie infused his songs with a warm, emotional honesty often missing from his recorded work. He sidestepped his icy synthesizer songs of the late '70s in favor of the soulful side of his repertoire, adding streetcorner touches of doo-wop and R&B beefed up by a gutsy three-man horn section.

And although there was a shortage of high-powered rock—he only did one song from his punky "Ziggy Stardust" album after doing six at his last Boston show in 1978—he compensated with a classy sophistication throughout.

Promptly at 7:30 pm, Bowie walked onto a gray, seemingly dull stage—even the scrim on each side was gray (covered by a bare hand on one side that seemed to be reaching toward a crescent moon covering the other)—but the bleakness was quickly erased with the opening song, "Look Back in Anger," a cry against dehumanization.

Bright blue lights then triggered "Heroes" (Bowie's light show was phenomenal, with special lighting cranes in the audience and a kaleidescope of stage lights reflecting off strips of gauzy shower-type curtains in the rear), while Bowie leaned back in his baggy trousers and wailed his melodic Walter Mitty tale about being a hero "for just one day."

Thus launched, the concert unfolded like a slice of cinema. For the romantic memories of "Golden Years," Bowie sat in a director's chair while his two singers, brothers Frank and George Simms, who were throwbacks to vaudeville in their ragtag, striped coats, stood beside him and pointed upward as though this were a Sha Na Na skit.

Bowie then hit stride during a segue from the grunting "Fashion" (which found guitarist Carlos Alomar romping out front for a solo aping the Count Five's "Psychotic Reaction") to his current summer hit "Let's Dance," a vastly overplayed funk tune that Bowie, to his credit, transformed via the line, "Put your red shoes on and let's dance the blues," as he angrily spit out the phrase and gave it new meaning.

A sultry portion followed with "Life on Mars" and "Sorrow" and then a campy reading of his recent love song "China Girl," with Bowie hugging himself in a mime gesture just before sliding to his knees to indicate his desire.

Razzle-dazzle footwork enhanced the comic paranoia of "Scary Monsters (and Super Creeps)," leading to some undulating pelvic grinds on "Rebel Rebel" during the verse "hot tramp I love you so." This in turn led to the night's only real surprise, an express-train romp through the old Velvet Underground song "White Light, White Heat," in which Bowie turned loose his band, notably the rave-up guitarist Earl Slick, who was last in town backing rockabilly star Robert Gordon.

Bowie's theatrical talents then came into play during the schizzy "Cracked Actor," as he spoofed Hollywood and Shakespeare's Hamlet by donning sunglasses and having a warped dialogue with a human skull he held aloft.

Only Bowie could make you wait in the rain to hear a dialogue with a skull. Truly, there seems no limit to his inventiveness.

Summary in this review includes a detailed description of the stage, the light show, the star's attire, and frequent mention of other bands and other performances. These huge events, attracting as many spectators as homecoming football games, are audience-participation concerts and designed to appeal to all the senses.

All elements of the review are present here; it is the summary that is expanded to include not only a listing of the songs performed, but also a description of other aspects of the performance. Opinion and identification are treated as they would be in any review.

One could say that a reader unfamiliar with David Bowie and his ilk would need some kind of dictionary to understand this report. But when artists such as this can attract more than 50,000 on a rainy night, and when their records, tapes, and compact disks sell as well as they do, most readers, certainly interested readers, need no further explanation.

Readers of reviews such as the Morse piece in the *Globe* often subscribe to publications specializing in a certain form of music (as *Rolling Stone* did in its early years). Such a publication was *The Illiana Beat*, a monthly newspaper dealing with rock and country-western. Knowing his readers, reporter Don Houser began a review of an Eric Clapton concert this way:[5]

CLAPTON DELIVERS COOL BLUES ON A HOT NIGHT

As the sun slowly sank into the western horizon, the Blasters took to Poplar Creek's stage to display their brand of rockabilly music. Originals from their Non-Fiction LP were interspersed with a few cover tunes from rock'n'roll's embryonic era, and were enthusiastically accepted by the audience. Playing for 50 minutes, the four-man unit continually cranked out music and wasted very little time with chatter.

The warm night air and the glistening stars overhead set the mood for the evening as the crowd anxiously awaited the arrival of the master of weeping guitars—Eric Clapton.

Looking better than he has in years, E.C. gave a stunning performance. Opening with "I Shot the Sheriff" the legendary guitarist brought the roaring crowd to its col-

---

[5]Courtesey of the *Illiana Beat*, August 1983.

lective feet. As the song progressed, something seemed different. Not only did Clapton appear more vibrant and healthy than in past years, but he once again had that gleam in his eye and that confident cockiness of days long past.

This specialized kind of writing is found in publications with limited scope, as opposed to newspapers with wide, diverse audiences. In this kind of review the writer assumes his readers are familiar with just about all aspects of his subject.

In popular music it has become common for all musicians to play more than one instrument; rare is the pop musician who does only one thing. Most sing, double in percussion, even on keyboard, woodwinds, and brasses. The review for a specialized publication would be content to simply name the players. The newspaper writer should also say what they played.

Defining the particular type of music a popular group plays is difficult because it is extremely faddish, and no sooner does one group come up with a new sound, or manner of dress, or stage appearance, than imitators are everywhere. Today's hottest record, today's top-drawing group, may well be forgotten tomorrow, because much popular music is also characterized by its impermanence.

But There Are Similarities

In spite of the considerable difference between a concert in Dallas' Cotton Bowl and one in Carnegie Hall in New York, there are similarities in the reviews of popular and classical music. Each should show balance in ensemble playing, and one performer should not overpower the others. When this happens in classical music, the blame lies with the conductor, whereas in pop the fault may be that of the sound engineer.

Regardless of the milieu, the performer should be accomplished on his or her instrument, and in each instance the audience is a factor.

Identification in popular music consists of the name and instrumentation of the group. It may not be necessary to name the players; it depends on how well-known they are, whether some or all have played in other groups, and perhaps how long they have been together. Some contemporary stars are better known than the group they happen to be with at the moment.

Mention of the success of the group in terms of recording should be included, as well as whether their songs are often done by other groups—a sure indication of superstardom. Summary will be mainly a description of the type of songs presented, with some breakdown as to which were fast, slow, vocal, or instrumental. Opinion is an evaluation of the success of the performance, based heavily on audience reaction.

Popular music is a comparative art form in that current groups are judged against other contemporary performers as a matter of course, not compared to long-standing musical standards. A review of a popular program often mentions other groups or other concerts as a basis for opinion, something that seldom happens with classical music, outside a few bastions such as the *New Yorker* and the *Christian Science*

Monitor. And in those instances, the comparison is made by critics. In popular music the reviewer is aware of other performers, and remembers what he himself has written in previous reviews, because readers remember. The writer covering popular music may spend even more time listening to recordings than his classical music counterpart.

Electronics Have Become a Factor

Because so much modern or popular music is electronic, an appreciation of electrical engineering is helpful. The sound system, either the one provided by the local sponsor or the one the performers bring with them, can make the difference between a successful and an unsuccessful program. Many genuine efforts have failed because the sound balance was wrong. It seems unfair to blame the group because a speaker went out in mid-song, yet one could say it is up to the group because it relies heavily on electricity, to make sure things are functional before the music begins.

One negative aspect about pop music concerts, at least from the standpoint of older people or occasional patrons, is audience behavior. Drugs and alcohol are often present. A mention of security arrangements is unfortunately often part of the advance story, as is an accounting of damage and destruction part of the review.

Some not particularly attuned to the popular music scene will wonder why anyone would want to go to such an event if the music cannot be heard, the performers are dim figures in the distance, and the air is unfit to breathe. The reply will be that the experience of being there, in the presence of the band and thousands (try 50,000) of others, is more important than what the band is playing. In a way this is a carryover of a 1950-1960s phenomenon called a "happening," where what goes on is not as interesting as who took part.

Ever since the incredible success—to say nothing of the impact on contemporary history—of the happening at Woodstock, many pop concerts have come to be regarded more as events of sociological and historical importance than performances.

The type of music a group is playing might be heavy metal, acid rock, punk, funk, new wave, or some hybrid form of contemporary music; the definition is probably important only to those who attend. The advance story can describe the act as favoring a certain kind of music, but the writer may be hard pressed to define just what the group is up to.

Since popular groups come with built-in labels about their brand of music, the best bet is to let them define or categorize themselves. This then can become a basis for comparing this group to others claiming the same characteristics.

Chapter Seven
Drama—Where "All the World's a Stage"

There is something universally appealing about theater, which is interesting because it is not the most popular of the arts. Not only do live theatrical presentations reach only a fraction of the film or television audience, there are no indications that the audiences will increase. This is a matter of logistics more than anything else. In spite of activity on Broadway, off Broadway, in community theaters across the land, at colleges and universities everywhere, the nature of live theater is limiting, because actors, directors, and craftsmen can only perform before a finite number at a time.

Theater companies at all levels seem to be fighting to retain the followers they have, rather than claiming new converts. Then why this feeling of familiarity with acting? Because it is a human activity anyone can relate to: "He was acting funny," or "she wasn't acting right." Consider the times the average consumer "goes into his act" when the price of meat is too high, when the dry cleaning isn't ready, when an offspring fails a responsibility, when the mechanic indicates a major overhaul is the only salvation for the 6-month-old car. The reader feels he or she knows about acting, even if he or she has little understanding of how it is done. Thus, the critic and reviewer begin their approach to drama with the contradiction that their readers know acting, but not the theater.

TWO WAYS TO LOOK AT IT

Dramatic criticism can be divided into two broad categories. These are the *physical* (or mechanical) considerations, and the *artistic* (or creative) ones.

Physical Considerations

Physical considerations deal with tangibles, with fixed objects, with the things that cannot be easily changed. The first of these is the stage itself.

It would help if all stages were alike, but they are not. A dramatic production could be presented on a stage wide enough to hold a symphony orchestra (or a junior high school basketball game), or in surprisingly narrow surroundings. The standard dramatic production takes place on a proscenium stage, where the audience sits in front of, and usually slightly below, the players. Because this is most common, a review would normally mention the stage only if it was not traditional.

If it is not proscenium it must be arena. Arena staging, both the oldest and the newest way to present dramatic action, has the audience on all four sides of the players. A modified version, with the audience on three sides, is called three-quarters arena, or three-quarters round. Some feel the biggest difference between proscenium staging and arena theater is the placement of the audience, but more feel it is the distance between players and audience that separates the two.

In many traditional houses the theater-goer nearest the stage may be 25 feet from the front of the playing area. In arena, the players often step over the feet of the audience. The distance separating them is down to nothing, and in most arena theaters, certainly those built for theater in the round rather than for other purposes, the most distant seats are not more than 12 or 15 rows back from the stage. An audience of 300 or 400 can all be within 50 feet of the action.

Because of this proximity in arena staging, design and direction take on increased importance. There can be no massive set pieces or walls on stage in arena, because they would block somebody's view, and furniture is low so that the audience can see over it. A door frame represents a door, and the actors must act as if an actual wall extends from it. Sets are more inclined to be suggestive than realistic. The complaint from traditionalists is that it is impossible to really act when there are no real sets, but others disagree, and say that the artificial restraints of the proscenium stage are what makes acting unbelievable. There is truth in each statement. A whisper in arena can indeed be a whisper, whereas a whisper on a traditional stage, a stage whisper, is a vocal trick designed to be heard 100 feet away.

The argument is that traditional theater cannot be realistic because everything is done for a comparatively distant audience, whereas in arena the actors can be quiet, secretive, or normal in speaking. Traditionalists will respond that that is what acting is all about, projecting emotions and sounds without losing the intensity of feeling.

Arena Fare Is Adapted.   Rarely is a play written expressly for the arena theater. Arena fare is normally adapted, and it follows that some plays adapt beautifully to arena and others do not. The reviewer needs to consider the suitability of a play to arena staging. A play where a principle actor ages considerably over the course of the action puts tremendous demands on the arena player because the proximity of the audience makes broad makeup impossible.

The lighting in arena is more like living room lighting; there are no footlights, often no powerful overhead lights. The entire stage is fairly well lighted, and age-lines drawn on an actor will look just like age lines drawn on an actor. But a "talky" play, where the emphasis is on conversation and vocal innuendo, can be far livelier on the round stage. This calls for skill on the part of the director.

Regardless of the staging, a major consideration is the audience. A standing-room-only crowd is certainly worth talking about, as is the presence of dozens of empty choice seats.

But the audience takes on a different aspect in a popular variation in staging, the dinner theater. This is more or less arena staging, but the audience is at tables, often finishing up dessert as Act One begins, presenting a different and unique consideration for the reviewer. One can hardly treat a dinner theater production in the same manner as a regular proscenium stage production if the audience is eating, drinking, and moving about to rest rooms. There is also the unusual seating, where many in the audience will have a better view of their dinner partners than the action. Dinner theater, at least so far, has meant light entertainment, a showcase for television and film stars, and no attempt at serious drama.

The Permanence of the Set

The next physical consideration is the set. There are three basic types of set for the traditional proscenium stage. The first is a permanent set, built by carpenters and electricians and designed to retain its efficiency for as long as a year without major repairs. The Broadway stage is the best, and perhaps the only, true example of this kind of set. Here the living rooms can be lived in, the appliances work, and staircases do not wobble. Even though the sets are changed they are structurally sound enough to last for eight shows a week for as long as a year. When a door slams shut the walls don't shake, windows are legitimate working windows, and pictures on walls are real pictures on walls, not paintings on walls of pictures.

A semi-permanent or traveling set for a first class touring company, called a national company, is almost as good. This is a set constructed either for a limited run, such as a 3-week revival of a classic from years past, or a set modeled after the permanent set of a Broadway show going on the road. Because this is a national company it will play only the larger cities where theaters will be well-equipped. The set will stay up for as short as a weekend or as long as a month or more, so when the stage hands set it up they know it will remain up for some time. It will be a sturdy set, although the emphasis is more on erecting and striking than on permanence. The set can be well-built, as on Broadway, but a major factor must be how easily it can be moved from city to city.

The least realistic set is not a set as much as a backdrop. This is used when funds run too low for a real set, or when a touring troupe is what is called a bus-truck company. These performers find themselves in high school gymnasiums and civic auditoriums more than on well-manned proscenium stages. The cast rides in the bus, the scenery is carried on a truck. The actors themselves reflect these varying levels of performance.

On Broadway one finds the Broadway stars. In the national company are actors of almost equal stature, in principal roles, certainly well-known to audiences everywhere. But the bus-truck companies are the unknowns. The leading actor may have some fans, or may be a moderately well-known TV personality, but for the most part this is where the unknowns break in, where the stagestruck and the less talented hope for a big break or satisfy their dramatic urges. No one gets very rich on the bus-truck tour. In such an instance the "set," such as it is, is more suggestion than actual entity.

The musical comedy "The Music Man" provides examples of these sets. During its long Broadway run the producers used regular library shelves, filled with real books, and put them on wheels so they could be rolled onstage and off for the library scene. When the students danced in and around the books they were, in effect, in a real library. It was partly for realism and partly for durability that the real thing was used. And of course it added to the effect when the student-dancers were able to take actual books out of actual bookshelves.

For the national company playing the big cities—Detroit, Chicago, San Francisco—the set had a couple of light-weight book shelves and some realistic looking book backs, the kind you can buy to fill up empty shelf space with famous titles—book backs, but no insides. There were only two such groups of shelves, and the students confined their dancing more to the front than behind and around the books. Still, there was a three-dimensional effect, and the audience could easily believe the action was taking place in a real library.

The bus-truck company that went to the smaller cities—Rockford, Illinois; Fargo, North Dakota; LaCrosse, Wisconsin—carried a minimum set. In this case, the playing area needs only one wall where a backdrop showing a library scene is unfurled. These road companies stay in a city for not more than one or two performances, so the hard-working crew sets up the stage, rests for two and a half hours or overnight while the show goes on, then takes it down, loads it on the truck and heads for the next town.

Other Physical Aspects

Lighting and sound are considerations that come in this general category. Some theaters use footlights, many use overhead lights, and most have spotlights in front of and offstage. The lighting should not be obvious, and normally is not part of a review unless it is markedly good or bad, or if there are certain special effects created by lighting (an explosion, a fire, police search lights) that are part of the action.

Sound can be a problem, particularly if microphones are used. Arena stage would find a grateful audience if for no other reason than one could hear the actors without amplification. Some proscenium theaters have microphones in the curtains, others use carefully placed floor mikes, still others put them on tables. The current trend is toward cordless microphones that can be attached to an actor's costume.

The last of the physical considerations is a kind of management matter. Many theater doors are distracting as they swing open and shut, sometimes noisily, usually allowing light and even sound to seep in from the lobby. That should not happen. It could be a construction problem or a greedy management willing to interrupt the action to get a few more paying customers into the house. Other theaters have problems with the noise of air conditioning, or noise from backstage, which again should not happen, or even traffic noise from outside. It is a rare theater indeed that is completely immune from the sound of airplanes overhead, and it is a rare actor who, having had a certain line continually hindered by low-flying aircraft, has not been tempted to look at his watch and say to the audience "right on time."

These are incidental factors, but they crop up just often enough for the writer to be wary. After all, his concern is the overall effect the theatrical offering has on the audience, and he is well prepared if he has considered all the things that might have a bearing on the success of the play. Even though the physical considerations are usually secondary to the artistic ones, this collection of theater and set and staging factors can be vital. They should be in the review if they have an effect on the play. Otherwise, the reader assumes that these matters were all satisfactory.

ARTISTRY ATTRACTS MOST ATTENTION

The emphasis of the review is almost always on the creative aspects of the offering, and probably begins with acting. The reviewer knows that in theater, the audience should feel that the actor is indeed the person he or she is playing, a good starting point, and is not walking through the part for the hundredth time. If that is the impression given then the actor has failed, unless it is an instance of someone like the late Yul Brynner, who made a career out of playing the lead in "The King And I." There the charm lay in the knowledge that he had been the King for more than a score of years. The audience did not want a fresh, new performance; it wanted to see the old Yul.

It is hard to imagine a theater review that does not discuss acting, directing, and writing. Acting normally occupies most of the reviewer's time, whereas the critic is more concerned with writing and direction, since in her arena the actors are usually well-known, and their particular talents well documented. The chances are that the critic is reviewing something being presented for the first time, whereas the average reviewer away from the big cities seldom judges a brand new enterprise.

When a review leads with and concentrates on the play itself, it is emphasizing the writing. Often the review begins this way because the play is a proven offering, and the players may be something less than skilled professionals. This is how Janna Anderson in Fargo handled a performance by a college group:[1]

---

[1]Courtesy of The Fargo *Forum*, Fargo, ND–Moorhead, MN, 1983.

'J.B.' NEW LOOK AT BIBLICAL STORY

By Janna Q. Anderson
Entertainment Editor

The production of "J.B.," now being staged at Concordia Theater is a serious, multilayered look at the question "Why me, Lord?"

Written by Archibald MacLeish, it's an updated and complicated version of the Biblical story of Job, rife with symbolism. J.B. is a guy who has everything going right. He has a beautiful wife and five children; a wonderful home; a successful business; and a blissful appreciation of it all. He believes God is unchanging.

Then God and Satan get into an argument. Counting on J.B.'s faith, God allows Satan to tempt him. J.B.'s children die in a war, an accident and by a harrowing murder. A bomb destroys all his material wealth, he becomes ill and his wife leaves him.

God himself said J.B.—Job—was "a perfect and upright man," and his destruction was "without cause." So, all that remains is the question, "Why?"

As MacLeish states in his forward to "J.B.":

"Job wants justice of the universe. He needs to know the reason for his wretchedness. And it is in those repeated cries of his that we hear most clearly our own voices. For our age is an age haunted and driven by the need to know."

Love is the overriding force that wins "J.B." in the end.

Directed by Concordia Theater instructor Helen Cermak, "J.B." raises its questions in an interesting staging. Don't attend this play looking for fancy sets and costumes. What's there is not much. Rather, attend to enjoy seeing one of the greatest Biblical stories in a new, different way.

Especially enjoyable in the performance are Mr. Zuss, played by Arthur Spiry, and Nickles portrayed admirably by Rooth Varland. These two characters play God and Satan in a sort of play within the play.

The only mess-up on opening night was technical trouble with an off-stage, echo chamber version of the real voice of God. It, as well as some snippets of music used in the performance, appear to be recorded—poorly recorded. There is no reason both those sounds couldn't have been done live. After all, this is live theater. The technical trouble with God's voice came at the most important point in the play. Most of these vital lines were muted, muffled and muddied.

"J.B." continues at Frances Frazier Comstock Theater with 8 p.m. performances through Monday.

This review is a little heavy on summary, and the opinion is based primarily on the writing. Notice that there is no mention of specific actors until the ninth (of 11) paragraphs. Had this been a high-priced professional production the writer would have commented on the sound failure much earlier in the review. However, in this instance of an amateur offering she did the right thing, which is to mention the failings, but not to imply that they ruined the evening.

The director's role is a challenge, both to the director and to the person writing about the direction. When it is perfect it is practically unnoticeable, putting the writer in the position of needing to praise what he cannot easily document. Good direction is marked by sensible action on stage. If an actor does something physically it should be motivated by the action of the play. Stage action should spring from, and reflect, the play itself.

Bad direction is marked by actors doing things for apparently no reason. When an actor gets up out of a chair, crosses the room, lights a cigarette, stands by a window, moves over in front of the fireplace, then sits down again, was there a reason for these actions? Did the dialogue have such power that any person would be compelled to move about the room? or was this a case of the director being afraid to leave a player sitting for too long a period of time, and thus manufactured, or created, action. It does not take a renowned critic to be able to make this distinction. Even the novice, after seeing a play or two, can determine if movement on stage was necessary or not.

This next review deals effectively with generally poor acting. Even though these are amateurs there is a modest charge for admission, and the audience should expect some level of ability:[2]

STUDIO PLAYERS LACK EMOTION IN 'RIV VU'

By Tom Carter
Herald-Leader Staff Writer

Studio Players have been plugging away at the craft of amateur theater for 30 years. They have good plays and bad plays. But that is the charm of amateur theater. Everybody has to start somewhere.

The Players' current production of 6 Rms Riv Vu, which opened last night at the Carriage House on Bell Court, is just that—a start.

In the Players' hands, 6 Rms Riv Vu could well be retitled Dull People Can Fool Around, Too, because the play is dispassionate to a fault.

The characterizations are shallow, almost plastic, and the play is more like a long, dull verbal essay than a play with action and turns in plot.

However, it must be pointed out that the opening-night audience had a pretty good time and had plenty to laugh at.

The comedy is the story of Anne Miller (Judith Cornelius) and Paul Friedman (Huett Tomlin), who come to inspect an apartment and find themselves accidentally locked there long enough to develop an attraction for each other.

They learn small, unimportant things about each other's lives. For example, he's no good at flirting. She's never known a man sexually except her husband.

The play alternates between moderately interesting exposition and slight developments in the action.

Once freed from the room, they lapse into a mildly giddy state of mind and return to the apartment later that evening for an innocent picnic together.

But even chasing this sort of innocence, Tomlin and Ms. Cornelius are not a convincing couple. They recite lines but don't seem to hear each other.

Tomlin, particularly, greets disappointment, elation and other turns of the plot with hardly a change in expression or attitude. He sounds more often like an insecure insurance agent than a prospective lover.

---

[2]Courtesy of the Lexington *Herald-Leader*, January 15, 1983.

Anne and Paul are shy, married people who are not in the habit of having to deal with passion that just suddenly decides to bloom. And when it does bloom, you have to take their word for it. Ms. Cornelius and Tomlin react as though they've been giving blood all afternoon and can't afford to risk passing out from excitement.

Their brief, supposedly intimate moments together are about as passionate as sorting laundry.

In smaller roles, Juanita Tecau brings a little life to the play as Janet, Paul's wife, and Stuart Silbar portrays Richard, Anne's husband.

Peggy Nichols portrays the elderly, nosy woman next door, though her costume—blouse, fitted skirt and easy walkers rather than a dowdy dress or something similar—doesn't allow her to carry off the image.

Charles Black plays the building superintendent, Eddie, with some semblance of a Puerto Rican accent. Also featured are Angie Krusenkalus and Frederic Zegelien as a couple who wander through the apartment a couple of times.

A singer, Shirley Sackville-West, performs some of her own compositions on guitar between scene changes.

★ ★ ★

Additional performances of 6 Rms Riv Vu will be at 8 p.m. today and 7 p.m. Sunday, then again the next two weeks at the Carriage House on Bell Court. Tickets are $5. Reservations: 259-0416.

The writer pointed out fairly high in the article (fifth paragraph) that the audience enjoyed the performance. Other than this, it is a very negative review, perhaps even heavy-handed. The writer does not mention a director, and the assumption is that the group (which we learn has been in business for 30 years) directs itself. The indication of ticket price and additional performances show that this is a fairly serious amateur group. Even in amateur theater there are degrees of skill, seriousness, and even professionalism. Because it is an amateur group the writer's criticism is mild at first—"are not a convincing couple"—then becomes more harsh—"Their brief, supposedly intimate moments together are about as passionate as sorting laundry."

A never-ending argument could be waged about the relative importance of writing and directing and acting. Without writing there is no play, only improvisation. Without acting there is no orderly presentation, only reading. Without direction there is no cohesion, only theatrical anarchy. Someone has to write the words, someone has to act the words, someone has to tell the actors what to do. At least in this chicken-and-the-egg argument we know which comes first, but we cannot generalize about which is most important.

Is there bad Shakespeare? Perhaps not, but Shakespeare has been done poorly. Is John Smith a great actor? Yes, but he has given poor performances. Is Jones an outstanding director? Admittedly, but he is better at drama than comedy.

And so it goes. Acting is both easy and difficult to assess, easy because anybody can have an opinion of an actor, difficult because that opinion must be documented. There need be some standards. Experience with real life and common sense are the benchmarks for critics and reviewers. A young actor plays an old person; does the action seem like that of old people the writer knows? An ingenue plays a love-stricken teenager. Is she realistic? Surely the writer has had at least passing experience with that emotion. If the person on stage is supposed to be athletic, does he or she move like an athlete? If the athlete is not believable the play fails.

Amateur actors across the country for years have courted hernia in Tennessee Williams' great "A Streetcar Named Desire," as aging Stanleys try to carry slightly overweight Stellas off stage. The director should realize that his or her leading man can barely get Stella off the ground, let alone carry her away. Let the director have the actor put his arm around the woman and walk off with her. That's sensible direction, and tends to add to the overall health of the cast.

Some college drama departments, believing that experience for student actors, directors, and technicians is more important than reality and believability, cast plays with only student actors, so that regardless of the range of ages in the roles, all the actors are within 3 or 4 years of each other in age. Other directors will seek professional actors for lead roles, particularly if the role is that of an older person, then fill out the cast with students. This, they feel, not only gives audiences a more believable performance, but also gives acting students the chance to share stage space with seasoned veterans.

Carter found much more to like when the University of Kentucky's drama department put on a successful modern play, which involved a blend of amateurs and professionals:[3]

ENERGETIC UK CAST ADDS SPARKLE TO 'FIFTH OF JULY'

By Tom Carter
Herald-Leader Staff Writer

For its final play of the summer, the University of Kentucky department of drama has put together a sparkling production of Lanford Wilson's Midwestern soap opera, Fifth of July.

The comedy-drama, which will be repeated tonight and next weekend at the Guignol Theater of the Fine Arts Building, comes highly recommended for a couple of reasons. The first is the cast, a bewitching combination of UK students and local professionals who have been molded with skill by director Joe Ferrell.

Another reason is playwright Wilson's success in having created a modern "family" of people tied together by much more 'than marriage, blood or accepted social structure.

There isn't much story. In fact, watching the Fifth of July is like sitting in a room full of happy strangers who interact now and then for reasons that take a while to make sense.

The play is set in 1977 at the farm home of Ken Talley (Roger Lee Leasor), who has several people visiting him for Independence Day weekend.

The visitors include some compatriots from the Vietnam years; Gwen, a singer, and her husband, John (Sue Grizzell and Michael Grice); Talley's sister, June (Sheila

---

[3]Courtesy of the Lexington *Herald-Leader*, June 25, 1983.

Omer), and her daughter, Shirley (Lizanne Lietzan); an aging aunt, Sally (Martha Bernier); Ken's lover, Jed (David Darst); and one of Gwen's groupies, a spaced-out guitar player, Weston (Tim McClure).

There are enough cross-plots, festering undercurrents and rampaging personalities to alternately confuse and bore anyone for the first hour of Fifth of July. But the play eventually settles down and is easy to follow in the second act.

Fifth of July is 2½ hours of bold character studies. Leasor, as the crippled, ex-hippie Ken, showcases his talent at going from giddy comedy to poignancy without missing a beat. Sue Grizzell as the frazzled singer is also a delight, though her dowdy costume is the pits.

Grice as Grizzell's weasel-like husband sets a high-energy pace and operates naturally at it. Lizanne Lietzan is a riot as a teenager out to drive everyone crazy with her whims.

Martha Bernier is outstanding in her portrayal of a 60-year-old woman. The role is particularly impressive since Ms. Bernier's last role at UK was as 14-year-old Juliet in Shakespeare's classic.

Rounding out the cast are Darst, who portrays Leasor's lover with just the right amount of subtlety and guarded feeling, and Ms. Omer, whose performance is only softened by some maddeningly mocking expressions.

Fifth of July is a fine way to while away a summer evening. The play, which is adult entertainment, reinforces Central Kentucky's strong corps of theater performers, who'd probably like nothing more than doing this sort of thing every night.

★ ★ ★

Additional performances of Fifth of July will be at 8 p.m. today, then again next Thursday through Saturday, in the Guignol Theater. For reservations, call 257-3297. Tickets are $5 for adults, $4 for students.

This is a good example of dramatic summary in the review. As Carter pointed out, the plot is not as important as the relationships among the characters, and is dismissed after the briefest mention. The reviewer praised the cast as a whole before singling out the leads, a credit to ensemble acting. Finally, there are negative comments in this review—one actress is criticized for her costume, and the first hour tends to be difficult to follow—but it is certainly a strong, positive review. Actually, it is unusual to find a review that has nothing negative to say. The Atkinson review of "Death of a Salesman" in chapter 3 is a rare exception.

There is no formula for the theater review, but the majority of leads are based on actors, because that is what is most obvious to the theater-goer. Actors have principal, or leading, roles; supporting roles; or character roles. There is no predetermined number of each, nor any rule that each must be present. There have been extremely successful two-person plays ("The Gin Game"), and plays with large casts ("Twelve Angry Men"). In most cases a person on stage is a leading player, a supporting actor, or a character actor. Or, as one student nicely summarized it, "Hero, best friend, town drunk."

In this review of the popular "Sugar Babies," William Glackin, writing for the

Sacramento Bee, had no doubts about either his lead or where the credit for the show's success belonged. Because this is for the most part a plotless event, notice how Glackin spends almost all his space on the performers:[4]

ANN MILLER, MICKEY ROONEY RETURN TRIUMPHANTLY
FROM BROADWAY STINT

By William Glackin
Bee Reviewer

SAN FRANCISCO—"Sugar Babies," which started here 4½ years ago, has come roaring back from its Broadway success, better than ever and even more incorrigible: tighter, brighter, funnier and—if possible—more magnificently and hilariously vulgar than before.

Best of all, it still has Mickey Rooney and Ann Miller leading the festivities.

Because Rooney seems more than ever a multiform genius and Miller is simply, well, Ann Miller—although indeed a wonderful and astonishing sight, tapping away on those remarkable legs and beaming with that same apple-cheeked face as if the 1940s had never left us—it is momentarily tempting to place him even higher as the one indispensable element in this success story.

But there is a moment toward the end of the show when they get together by themselves for a little dueting, Rooney at the piano and then the two of them dancing together, when you suddenly realize that not only does the show need both of them but in a way they need and serve each other. She gleams perfection, every smile and step in place; he's a raffish, unpredictable mess, an uncalculated, incalculable delight. They are foils; they set each other off perfectly.

The show remains both a burlesque show and a tribute to and history of the form. It is based on author Ralph G. Allen's scholarship as well as affection; some of the numbers listed in the program even have historical footnotes. It is full of wonderfully terrible jokes, most of them old and redolent with sexual references; it also includes some classic old comedy routines.

It is also full of pretty women, most of whom, by some strange mistake, are pretty well covered up. It is true that burlesque began in the 19th century in tights, but they were discarded in the 20th. These lovely young women jiggle a little, but they are hardly ever even partially bare. What is lost is not titillation but tease—one of the chief delights of burlesque. Sally Rand in a body suit, or something like it, is thus reduced to mere prettiness without the fun; impersonating her, Carol Ann Basch moves her ostrich feather fans with admirable grace, but the adolescent thrill is gone.

This grumble aside, I'm happy to admit I was laughing twice as much as I did the last time.

Rooney doesn't do it all. There are three sterling veterans to help with the hilarity— Mickey Deems, Maxie Furman and Milton Frome—as well as Jay Stuart to function as a superb straight man and an excellent singer and the spectacularly beautiful Gail Dahms (taking Ann Jillian's place) in several key spots, most notably in "Monkey Business," in which she rattles off one of those classic burlesque patterns to perfection.

---

[4]Courtesy of the Sacramento *Bee*, October 29, 1983.

There is no "bad" language in the show, in case you're wondering, but the double meanings are so unmistakable that describing them could get me reported to the Ombudsman. Somehow, though, they do not give offense. In some cases, both their obviousness and their age are part of their charm:

Furman: I'm working over at the woman's bloomer factory.
Frome: Is it a good job?
Furman: I'm pullin' down about 50 a week.

Bob Williams and his great dog have left the show, but the loss is more than made up by two young men of sensational talent and skill, both of whom happen to come from the Bay area. Frank Olivier, who is only 22, is a juggler who works with the traditional tenpins, torches and unicycle; what he does is brilliantly good, but it is how he does it—the happy, innocent, unsophisticated air he projects—that makes him irresistible, the most lovable juggler in memory. Ronn Lucas, who is surely the greatest ventriloquist to come along since Senor Wences, is remarkable not just for his technical skill and timing (he does echoing voices, among other things) but even more for the way, working toward the end of his act with just his bare hands, he moves us onto an almost surreal level, in which these various parts of his body begin to take on independent life.

They both won ovations.

And then there's Mickey Rooney. Much of the time his style is swift, loose, outrageous in its extravagance, but the timing is unerring, and the wicked gleam in his eye shines with the brilliance of a mind sensing every subtle thing that's happening. The funniest sustained thing he does remains Francine, an aging beauty in a platinum wig and a wild orange dress.

And then there's that brief moment at the piano. when he plays with the flash of a professional accompanist and the beauty of a born musician, and sings Jimmy McHugh's "I Can't Give You Anything But Love" with such gravelly, tender perfection, that you may suddenly realize how many Mickey Rooneys there are, including the one who gave us the great depiction of the middle-aged, retarded Bill in the unforgettable television show of that name, and you think: My God, this crazy man is a genius.

The review has a strong opening and a matching close, which includes a mention of Rooney's other work. This is another way the writer can express the idea that it is the performers, rather than writers or directors, who are the main attraction. The reviewer is warm in his praise of Ann Miller, but still leaves no doubt that Rooney is the main event.

Normally the leads are on stage most of the time, have more dialogue than others, and are simply more important to the play. Supporting players are just that; their task is to make the leads look good. The leads could do something with the theme of the play without supporting actors, but the supporting actors are worthless without the leads. They should be judged accordingly. Character roles are for comic relief, to provide contrast to leads and supporting roles, and occasionally to provide a certain bit of business that can not be comfortably done by other players. This is how they should be criticized.

The writer covering theater should know if the assignment is drama, comedy, tragedy, farce, whether it is designed to be allegorical, what the period is, what the playwright's intentions were. A lack of this kind of advance information can be serious. The extremely successful Albee play of the early 1960s, "Who's Afraid of Virginia Woolf?" was a fine modern tragedy, and achieved success in New York, on film, and on the road. It is still frequently performed. But the writer seeing it for the first time may be surprised at the amount of laughter generated in the first act. In that part, before the action becomes bitter, Albee has created sparkling dialogue. The writer who is aware of this has a better overall viewpoint then the one not sure if he is seeing a comedy or a tragedy.

The writer dealing with live theater needs to get as much advance information about a production as he can, not to make him appear to his readers as a theatrical expert, but because he really has a very serious charge. He is telling those who have yet to see the performance what they can expect to find, and he is telling those who saw it why they did or didn't like it. The entertainment writer tells his readers this is the tenth different production of a certain play in which this lead actor has played a part, which is why he is so at ease with it; or he tells them that another actor is a last-minute replacement. The audience leaves the theater satisfied or unhappy, then reads the newspaper for reasons. The more informed the writer, the better the readers are served.

Chapter Eight
Music Plus Theater
Equals Dance

The critic rejoices in the dance. A program of ballet or modern dance makes her week. Where else could one find this combination of color and movement, of athletic ability and grace, of music and drama, of poignancy, poise and wonderfully timed pratfalls. Music and theater meet on the stage; what a delight. To top it off, the audience she will sit with is inclined to be more informed, more sophisticated, and more culturally aware than gatherings at live performances of other arts.

That's the critic. The reviewer, however, fresh from covering a foreign film, a new wave pop group, and a touring musical, may evidence more apprehension than anticipation. His knowledge of the dance, at least at first, may extend barely beyond what he has seen on television, and that experience is subject to television's propensity for showing only the faces, or upper bodies, of dancers.

For him it is perhaps a trip back to the basics, to see what this ancient, traditional, yet exciting medium is all about.

Dance combines music of some form with some kind of theater, or at least some kind of theatrical expression. Dance is planned movement, presented on a stage, and accompanied by either live or recorded sound. At its simplest it is movement to sound. At its most complex it is a combination of music, theater, athletics, emotion, and expression. It can be a great deal of fun for the new reviewer, but it can also be frightening.

An examination of dance begins with music and theater. How well they come together is usually the key to the success of a dance program. If the music seems to fit the dancing, or the dancing fits the music, and if a feeling or a story or a message is conveyed, and if there is skill and talent and creativity displayed, the program is successful.

Dance is an old medium and is continually re-examining its past. Ethnic or national groups are interested in preserving their traditional culture through dance. Music may indeed be the universal language, but dance is not far behind.

NEW AND OLD CHOREOGRAPHY

There are basically two kinds of choreography—traditional and modern. The dancers are either performing according to traditional concepts, or are modern and innovative, introducing their own concepts. That is, traditional dancers perform according to existing standards, and modern dancers establish their own standards. A dance program can be traditional in that the dancers can be actually performing the same dance—the same set of movements—that has been done many times before, or they can be using traditional dance movements and steps in a new composition.

Traditional dance steps and movements are now recorded in a kind of shorthand called *labanotation*, a method of showing the body of the dancer as a stick figure of sorts, with arms and legs and head in various positions that correspond to traditional ballet steps. Earlier, the classic positions and movements were laboriously passed from generation to generation in longhand. By following the choreography of an earlier century, a modern traditional dance company can perform a classical ballet almost exactly as it was done 100 years ago.

Early choreographers, as they passed along instructions about music, included the speed at which it should be played, showing how dancers are to move and step at each point in the music. There is room for interpretation in recreating these dances, just as there is room for interpretation in theater and music. But it is also possible, in dance as in theater and music, to give a performance virtually identical to one presented many years ago. This is how such classics as ''Swan Lake'' and ''Giselle'' are recreated.

Choreographers designing new ballets, or new dances to be performed to old music, often choose to stage a traditional form of dance, using basic ballet positions and movements. Similar activity goes on in modern dance, where a choreographer can recreate any other modernist's program through labanotation.

Modern dance can be extremely acrobatic, can be done in a variety of costumes, and can be quite different from traditional dance. It can be based on native dances, as some modern black groups practice; it can be European ethnic, South American, American Indian, or oriental in concept. It is almost an art with no rules; nobody prescribes how long a dance program or a certain dance must be.

The complete ballet occupies a full evening of dance, but it can be a long or a short evening. No one indicates how few or how many performers there should be. The accompaniment can range from one tom tom to a symphony orchestra. Dancers can dance to drums, wood blocks, even handclapping and foot stamping. There can be any combination of men and women. Thus, the first step for the new reviewer is to recognize this almost complete lack of limitations.

GETTING READY FOR THE FIRST ASSIGNMENT

The reviewer's first challenge could be a traditional ballet, performed by amateurs or professionals, a modern dance group, or a group presenting folk dances. Even the more experienced writer will probably not have seen the group or program before, unless it is a well-known ballet such as "The Nutcracker," or if it has been presented on television. Where the dance was first presented, and by whom, is part of basic identification in the review, and is offered as information, not opinion.

If the group is called a modern dance company it either has an ethnic background, or is simply a modern group using contemporary movements and themes. Program notes and publicity releases help here, as long as the reviewer remembers that the releases say what the troupe hopes to do, and there is no guarantee it will be as successful as the release indicates. At least the notes show what goals the company has set for itself.

Identification, summary, and opinion form the basis for the dance review. Because the art is not as familiar to most readers as music, film, theater, or television, the opening statement may be primarily explanatory, with supporting opinion coming later.

The following reviews are typical of those produced by most reviewers, meaning those assigned to a features or amusements staff who find themselves evaluating a variety of artistic activities. They contain much more explanation and basic description than in reviews of the more familiar arts.

In the first example, Janna Anderson greets the performance of a local company as an old and welcome friend. In this instance, as most of the artists are amateurs and the company seems to perform well within itself—meaning that it does not attempt activities beyond its ability—the writer concentrates on summary blended with opinion. When it appeared in print, this review was preceded by basic identification, including principals and soloists, in agate type.[1]

AREA ARTISTS SHINE IN 'ON STAGE' DANCE PRODUCTION

by Janna Q. Anderson
Entertainment Editor

Sweet, then high-spirited—that's "On Stage," the Red River Dance and Performing Company production now being presented at North Dakota State University's Festival Hall.

The area's top dance company inaugurates its first three-show dance season with a first act that seems hesitant and a second act that leaps out and grabs its audience, carrying it along and building energy to an entertaining high.

The first segment of the 80-minute show is a tribute to love titled "Affairs of the Heart." It's set in a park, with a lone balloon vendor (Chris Breitling) tying its nine

---

[1]Courtesy of The Fargo *Forum*, Fargo, ND–Moorhead, MN, September, 1983.

movements together. Depicted in smoothly characteristic dance are an elderly couple, a group of teen-agers, a solitary woman, a young career couple, a love triangle and an adult couple.

Janet Dickerson performs a lyrically gentle, sweeping solo dance in this act. Dannul Dailey and Lisa Nelson pair off well as the career couple, executing a number of difficult lifts and leaps with graceful ease. Lynda Olson Demke and David Demke are perfectly matched in another dance duet.

One of the great things about the RRD&PC has always been its use of local musicians, composers and arrangers. This show's score is almost completely made up of original material by area artists. David Hanson wrote most of the clean, upbeat pop music for "Affairs of the Heart." Rick Kasper and Paul Severson also made contributions.

This excellent music is performed live in fine fashion by vocalists Vicki Klipfel, Curt Monteith and Carol Wolsky, and by a pit orchestra. It's a professional job all the way around.

While the first act has its bright moments, it seems piece-meal and slow-moving. The second act is an entirely different animal—jazzy, dynamic, packed with fun.

The highlight of the show is the opening number of the second act, "Uptown, Downtown," a dance piece with a great original score by Henry Gwiazda. It shows off what an outstanding choreographer like Eddie Gasper can do with a spare set and a few talented dancers.

The piece starts out with five street kids (Dailey, Demke, Ryan Myrold, Grant Norman and Bob Richard) silently whiling away the day on the front stoop of a tenement. It slowly builds to a clever beat, gradually unleashing the raw energy of these young toughs and channeling it into a fantastically flashy tap series.

It's as if these guys just discovered they could dance. The audience continually burst into spontaneous applause during this particular performance on opening night.

As this tap number continues, the dancers move into an arcade, complete with video-games and the whole teen scene. The dance takes on greater effect as it reflects youthful society.

Exciting. Humorous. Thought-provoking. Wildly entertaining. It doesn't get any better than this.

The finale of "On Stage" is titled "Lullabye of Broadway." To music arranged by David Ferreira, this dance sequence also employs tap—this time with the entire company working its way all over the the stage in glitzy white costumes. It's an exhilarating finishing number for a rewarding, heartwarming evening of entertainment.

In this review, Anderson correctly used lay terms such as *leaps* and *lifts* to describe the action. She also included a brief history of the group as part of identification, as she described the company's habit of using local talent.

In this next review of a Joffrey Ballet program, *The Sacramento Bee*'s William Glackin also faced a contemporary, rather than traditional, performance. His task was made difficult in that there was little mention of the nature of the dance in the program. Notice in the fifth paragraph he wrote that one dancer "might be regarded as the Angel of Consolation." In using this language he correctly avoided appearing presumptuous, as he would if he made the announcement that the dancer was the Angel, information that others in attendance did not have.

In dance, unless it is all modern and innovative, the reviewer should give some background, not only about the performers, but about the dances they are presenting. This is how Glackin wove this into his review:[2]

JOFFREY BALLET SHOWS TREMENDOUS RANGE, ELOQUENCE

By William Glackin
Bee Reviewer

SAN FRANCISCO—The various styles of dance started taking in each other's washing long ago. Modern dancers were always classically trained, of course; ballet companies finally loosened up and began to absorb a little modern. Now a work in one style often has more than a touch of the other. And all to the good. A greater vocabulary helps lead to eloquence—if you've got something to say.

The Joffrey Ballet, ending its first week in the Opera House, has plenty to say and perhaps the most flexible and comprehensive vocabulary in dance. Traditionally, it is No. 3 among American dance companies, yielding precedence to New York City Ballet and American Ballet Theater. But when it comes to range, it yields to no one.

Thursday's program was a good example, with Laura Dean's "post-modern" "Night," works from the 1930s by Frederick Ashton and Kurt Jooss that still seem unconventional, and Gerald Arpino's new "Round of Angels," which seems nothing else but pure Arpino.

Twelve intense minutes long, it appears to be about loss, grief and consolation, and is dedicated to the memory of James R. Howell, for 20 years a member of the Joffrey, mostly in musical capacities, who died last October at the age of 46. I say "appears to be," because the dedication is the only note in the program. But the general drift of the ballet seems clear, and is also emotionally quite powerful.

Out of a group of low-lying, writhing dancers on a dimly lit stage, two men arise in anguish, one holding the other, who presently runs quickly off. The bereft one (James Canfield) turns to find a slim female figure (Patricia Miller) and when the others leave, they perform a kind of duet-in-place, very close together, lovely moves in which she might be regarded as the Angel of Consolation.

There is a solo for him, and another duet which now moves around the stage, as five men circle the pair, often raising their arms like wings. They carry her off briefly and he sinks in grief again, but she returns, to be lifted up too, as the curtain falls.

Canfield and Miller danced the leads with arresting strength and beauty of line, and richly deserved their ovation.

The show began with a modern classic, Ashton's "Les Patineurs (The Skaters)," which he made in 1937 for the Vic-Wells (later Sadler's Wells, still later the Royal Ballet) with Margot Fonteyn and Robert Helpmann in leading roles.

This time it was the warm, smooth, lovely, elegant Denise Jackson in the major duet (with Philip Jerry) and it was the engaging Mark Goldweber, a leaper and spinner of spectacular, springy strength and precision, who galvanized the audience into excitement with his brilliance.

---

[2]Courtesy of the Sacramento *Bee*, July 15, 1983.

There was plenty of bright, whirling excellence, too, from Cameron Basden, Lauren Rouse, DeAnn Duteil and Charlene Gehm, but the central charm of the work remains the choreography of Ashton, whose subtle and often witty blend of ballet style and skating style, each altering the other until the distinctions become a happy blur, seems as fresh as ever.

Laura Dean's "Night" followed "Les Patineurs" by 43 years, but the two works are surely light years apart. About 15 minutes long, "Night" might be descrbed as "Minimalist" in the sense that the word has been applied recently to the kind of music that features a steady pulse, lots of percussion, simple harmonies, insistent repetition and only small, gradual changes.

Dean's score, her own music, is in this style, sounding like tapes of piano chords heavily dubbed over each other. It is unrelievedly loud, hammeringly percussive and eventually oppressive. The choreography, for an ensemble of eight clad in black Japanese-style pajamas, resembles the music in structure but is not oppressive, only not very interesting. Simple moves are repeated with small changes. But the dancing grows increasingly active, and obviously requires notable energy and skill, which it got from these performers.

Kurt Jooss' scathing indictment of war and the governments that create war, "The Green Table," is another classic, dating to 1932. Its scenes have been described before—the gesturing diplomats, the dominating figure of Death, dressed as a warrior, the doomed figures of Young Soldier, Young Girl, Old Mother, (rebellious) Woman and Profiteer—but the images have lost none of their power.

Philip Jerry, stamping out Death's moves like a monstrous machine, drove home the theme inexorably, and Luis Perez as the leering profiteer, Denise Jackson as the Mother and Carole Valleskey as the Girl were especially eloquent.

By contrast John Hurst, Glackin's colleague on the *Bee*, drew what could seem like an impossible assignment. He was to review "The Nutcracker," probably the most popular, familiar, and seasonal ballet of them all. Each year the Sacramento orchestra presents it, just as each year at Christmas there are thousands of performances of "The Messiah." These are events that deserve the critical attention of every newspaper, yet they are so well-known and tested by time that it is often difficult to find something to say that hasn't been said over and over. Hurst solved this annual puzzle nicely by presenting a kind of feature-review:[3]

'NUTCRACKER'S' DANCERS DELIGHT YOUNG AUDIENCE

By John V. Hurst
Bee Reviewer

Can't take the kids to Disneyland for Christmas? Take heart. Take them instead to Sacramento's Community Center Theater, where tours of our very own, very special Magic Kingdom are currently being conducted practically every day.

We're talking about Tchaikovsky's Christmas ballet, "The Nutcracker," whose

---

[3]Courtesy of the Sacramento *Bee*, December 9, 1983.

16th annual production by the Sacramento Ballet and Sacramento Symphony opened Thursday for a seasonal run of 17 performances. And to say there's magic here is to state the case exactly.

How else explain a houseful of attending moppets so attuned to the proceedings at Thursday's opening they'd cheer and applaud in all the right places (and cheer they did), yet so engrossed they'd settle right back into rapt silence, each time, for the rest?

And what else but magic can explain a ballet so delightfully explicit and accessible it was possible to follow the action—even the Clara's-dream story line—without so much as a glance at the synopsis?

The questions may sound rhetorical, but there are elements of this "Nutcracker" that suggest answers. First, Carter Nice conducts the orchestra at a volume calculated to encourage silence in the seats, as well as at a pace slow enough to help clarify things instead of hurrying the movement.

Second, the choreography, adapted by artistic director Barbara Crockett-Gallo from Lew Christensen's original, gives a very human scale and style to the dancers' movements and mime, communicating their interactions—those between the children in the party scene, in a notable example—in ways that are as immediately recognizable as they are enjoyable.

Finally, the costumes by Don Ransom and the imaginative, two-dimensional sets by Leonard Weisgard and David West add lots of mesmerizing color to go with the equally mesmerizing movement and music.

Many of the ballet's principal roles are shared by more than one dancer during a given run—Kevin Lee and Ian Twiss alternate, for instance, in the dual role of Herr Drosselmeyer's nephew and the Nutcracker Prince—so the fact that a reviewer sees only those in the opening performance goes with the territory.

Still, it's appropriate to mention some of the opening's standouts. And besides the obvious ones—the aforementioned Lee, Dianna Yee as the Dancing Doll and the Snow Queen, Monica Mudgett as a Sugar Plum Fairy equally stunning in movement and appearance, Duncan Schute as the Cavalier and Robert Nichols as the Snow Prince—there are some real attention-getters among members of the corps who have grown into some of the featured roles.

And not the least of these is young Kira Kay in the role of Clara, the girl whose sugar-spun dreams fuel this ballet. A 13-year-old who has practically grown up in the corps, one who has advanced through successive "Nutcracker" productions to this, her second turn as Clara, she is a twinkling presence who dances with light, lithe fluidity and manages to project a palpable personality as well.

There are some especially excellent turns, too, by Karin Wertz as the Senorita, David Jursich as el Toro, Michael Dwyer as the boy in the "Turkish Delight" number and Bonny Baldwin as the Rose.

Still, the dance duet by Mudgett and Schute, as Sugar Plum Fairy and her Cavalier, was the opening's best-of-show. And this despite the fact that the spirited, athletic "Dance of the Russian Trepak" by Matthew Devore, Don Sparks and Lee Wigand drew even louder cheers from the opening's young audience.

You can bet, with the kind of standards evident here, that the dancers appearing in alternate performances will be every bit as good as the ones who made the opening.

Not only is this a positive, cheerful review, it is unabashedly promotional. That approach would correctly be challenged if the offering had been a new performance, but not for the 16th annual appearance of an old favorite.

This is the kind of review of a traditional effort that reassures the reader that things are well as always in the fantasyland of the Nutcracker.

When it comes time to write, one of the first concerns has to do with the music. The reviewer must know if the music is ballet music or some other musical form that has been adapted for dance. The composer may have had in mind dancers and a certain story line, as in classical ballet; or a choreographer, feeling that a piece of existing music suggested certain physical activities, may have created a ballet to go with it.

The review should say if the music is performed by a live group or orchestra, or if it is recorded. Ballet is not a good revenue-producing business and many companies cannot afford the luxury of live musicians. A consideration of the music, or lack of it, comes in the identification part of a dance review. Similarly, if the sound is a positive or negative factor it can add to the writer's opinion, as long as he is able to determine who should be blamed for poor sound, or praised for effective use of recordings.

There should be some indication of the size of the company, the number of dances it presented, and the general training and background of the dancers. It is important to know if a premier dancer has danced that role before, just as it is important to know if an actor has played a part before, or if a violin soloist has performed a certain concerto before.

What They Wear, Where They Dance

Another part of the review has to do with costumes, either the traditional leotards and tutus, or some other form of dress. Some mention should also be made of the dance area, but the writer needs to be careful here. Dancing is an energetic activity, combining athletic ability and grace. There are few stages constructed specifically for dance. In most instances, the dance company must adapt, and must make slight or major changes depending on the conformation of the house. Dancers must be flexible in more ways than one.

Dance as an art form can be as delightful and artistic as any of its companions. Surely no other art can match classical ballet for sheer grace, and there is something to be said for having something to watch while listening to great music. At the highest levels, such as the Bolshoi Ballet or widely accepted American companies like Katherine Graham or Alvin Ailey, the product can be appreciated by anybody. Certainly the emergence of several extremely gifted but also extremely masculine dancers in the 1970s and 1980s—notably Edward Villella and Mikhail Baryshnikov—has helped. They are among those who have become media stars, and have achieved fame and recognition considerably beyond the comparatively narrow confines of dance. They have gone a long way to help remove the misplaced notion that dance is for the effeminate, for those who could not make the football team.

The area of dance provides a challenge for the performer and the writer. Many beginners tend to become overly conservative when faced with the assignment of covering dance, because they know there will be some in the audience who know more about the art then they do. This is an unnecessary fear. The reviewers cited in this book faced their first dance assignment with no real expertise in the field, but were able to present an adequate review based on providing identification, summary and, as much as possible, opinion. As they became more experienced they realized that the unfamiliar art quickly disappears, to be replaced by the excitement of a new evening of dance. The reviewer, then, emulates the critic, and similarly becomes a fan.

Chapter Nine
Design and Function Meet in Architecture

The reason for including architecture in a book on reviewing may seem to be more historical than practical. Architecture is among the oldest of the traditional arts, and still one of the most interesting. Here a great architect can make a name with one outstanding design; yet even those close to the art, and this would include most reviewers, probably have trouble listing even a dozen great names in architecture.

This field obviously calls for a great deal of artistic ability and creativity, but as a practical matter the typical reviewer will enjoy a long and productive career without ever getting to write about it.

If one were to list critics specializing in the various arts, architecture would have the shortest roster. There are able critics who specialize in other arts who have done very well in the criticism of new designs and buildings, but those who concentrate on architecture could probably be counted on the fingers of one hand. When the time comes that a new architectural concept needs evaluation, a fine arts specialist is likely to get the call. But in the event a fine arts specialist is not available, the general purpose reviewer may suddenly be faced with a new challenge. It need not be a formidable one.

A MATTER OF CATEGORIES

In the broadest possible terms the architect's concerns can be divided into three categories: public buildings, private buildings, and residences. As a subcategory there are shopping centers, although the commercial considerations there tend to overpower artistic appreciation. That is, the matters of access to stores, parking, delivery, and maintenance, to say nothing of the overall theme or style, can limit originality.

89

Public buildings are city halls, libraries, courthouses, hospitals, and school and university buildings. They are characterized by being funded, usually, with public money, and by being designed for use by a general public, so funding and planned use are the primary concerns of the architect, and are therefore subjects of the review.

Private buildings are office towers or complexes financed by private money, often provided by insurance companies and banks, designed for the private use of tenants. Frequently they are specifically designed for the unique needs of a certain tenant. Becuase the funding is private rather than public, they tend to be grander, more opulent, and more luxurious than public buildings.

Private residences are designed with the terrain, the size of the family, and the family's particular or peculiar interests and personalities in mind. The basis for criticism is originality and function, given the purpose of the building or residence.

Architecture is judged on design and function, and the two are treated equally. A marvelous design but a complete lack of function is not an architectural success. An extremely functional building with no aesthetic appeal is little better. Unfortunately many public buildings, where funding is limited, turn out to be functional but not at all attractive. The limitations placed by budget and usage often insure more attention to function than design.

DESIGN IS THE ARTISTIC ELEMENT

Design is a purely artistic concept. The critic looks at the scope of the building, the sweeping lines, shadows, high points, balconies, setbacks, and the use of materials. Moving inside she deals with wall and floor and ceiling materials, entryways, and lighting. A new 50-plus story building may be some 800 to 900 feet high, and the architect has the opportunity to create an 800-foot line, a sweep of glass and steel a half block long, a facade twice the size of a football field.

This designer can also call for glass and chrome and steel panels to catch the afternoon sun, and to pick up the glow of morning. Or he or she can conceive of a strong, granite wing epitomizing solidity and strength. The exterior design of a building can be extremely suggestive, and can give feelings of strength, color, and grace. This is pure design; this is creating sky castles, turning fantasy towers into reality, constructing spires that reach the sky or, as some writers have put it, scrape the bottoms of the airlanes.

Other important considerations in a new building are the size and location of windows, observation towers, platforms and decks, spires, and entrances. Most people walk in and out of doorways ranging in height from 7 feet at their home or apartment to perhaps 15 feet in a large public building. Imagine the excitement in creating an entryway 30 feet tall, twice as high as need be, but created for a certain artistic effect. This is worth writing about.

The design of a building makes a statement. A bank building should reflect solidity and trust, a theater should be graceful, and an insurance tower should be solid but not too lavish. Doors should work at City Hall, and there should be good sound proofing in a library. In blending the intangibles of trust, mood, or feeling with the basic function of the edifice, the architect is indeed a creative artist.

An architect can design an atrium with living trees in a new office building, bringing the outdoors, literally, indoors. Some hotels—an interesting combination of public buildings built with private money—have lobbies that reach the roof. Think about the vision an architect showed when he or she first suggested a lobby with a ceiling 300 feet above ground level. Glass walls, both interior and exterior, some reflecting, some opaque, provide interesting combinations of visibility and privacy.

There can be different levels on a floor, where a visitor steps down three steps, or up three steps, to a certain area. These are strictly artistic considerations. The function of an area may remain the same, but the feel of it can be enhanced by letting people walk up or down. The architect is always aware of what people in the building, as well as outside, will see.

NOW, DOES THE BUILDING WORK?

Function is the basic, gritty aspect of architecture, and it simply means, ''Does the building work?'' The architect deals with building use, and takes into account how many people will be entering and leaving at the same time, and how many will be using stairs, corridors, or swinging doors. There are elevators, restrooms, storage areas, heating and air conditioning, trash removal, laundry considerations, and food service, if it is that kind of building, among the functional areas.

University buildings have unique problems in terms of restrooms, because the bulk of the restroom activity will take place in the few minutes between classes. Water is a part of any building, and water tends to leak, or to gurgle. More than one early television studio had a major design flaw in that when toilets were used, and the pipes went near recording areas, sensitive microphones picked up the unwanted sound. Similarly, when a business uses many computers and other pieces of modern office machinery, it can present a temperature control problem.

TOO MANY THINGS TO WRITE ABOUT

Because it may be impossible to judge such matters on the basis of models and drawings, the functional aspect is more guess than certainty in the initial review. Still, it can, and should, be discussed.

How the building looks and how it works form the basis for architectural criticism, which seems simple, but it is not. The building may have close to 1 million square feet of floor space, may involve materials brought from the far reaches of the world, may be furnished in a dozen different areas by a dozen different interior designers, and is to be occupied by a diverse collection of professional people.

There are enough factors to consider in a major office building designed for public use to fill a book. The best method is to select representative considerations, good or bad, and let them be the basis for opinion. The exterior design is necessary in an architecture review, as is a description or evaluation of the function. After that it is a matter of careful selection, and the writer must decide which, among the thousands of things that could be said, need to be said.

A building worth reviewing is announced by the architect and the tenant together, and they supply the press with drawings, elevations, and scale models. These form the basis for the review, which of necessity concentrates on design. There was an interesting development in the erection of Houston's Pennzoil Place, two trapezoidal buildings joined at the base, designed by the famous Johnson–Burgee team. The design, in two-dimensional and model form, was so intriguing that prospective tenants began lining up. So great was the interest that the buildings, originally designed to be 34 stories tall, were expanded upward to 36 stories. However, this is clearly the exception. Most buildings upon completion will be exact duplicates of the architect's models.

The interior of a building can be judged by itself. There should be harmony between adjacent rooms, and there should be color and texture coordination from one area to another. The furniture, the art work adorning the walls, even statuary, are planned to be part of an entire interior feeling. The parts of the interior should relate to each other, and there should be contrasting and similar elements.

But outside is a different matter. Here the architect loses some control. He is charged with designing a building that will look attractive not only as it stands alone, or as it is seen alone, but in relation to surrounding buildings. Ideally, each building enhances its neighbors, but that is not always the case.

There are some striking examples of this aspect in the world, notably the famous Alamo in Texas and the even more famous Leaning Tower of Pisa. Each is among the most photographed of buildings, yet invariably the photographs show only the building in question. A personal visit reveals that each is surrounded, even dominated, by larger or more imposing structures.

The factual elements of architecture are relatively easy to deal with, but the aesthetics are something else. This is what separates the critical review in the arts section, dealing with the artistry of the object, from the routine report on the business page, more likely to be concerned with leasing arrangements, square footage, and tenants.

TAKING A LOOK AT THE PRIVATE SECTOR

Now the writer comes to what can be a pleasant aspect of this infrequent role as architecture critic, a chance to report on a private home. This is a blend of the architect's skill with the needs and desires of the client. Not all homes must be three bedroom, two bath, two-car garage. Some expensive houses have indoor swimming pools, some have huge boulders as part of the house, with appropriate thanks to

Frank Lloyd Wright; some make extensive use of native woods, some have many different levels of flooring.

Some are built in the form of a complete circle, whereas others are like an old-time fort, with living quarters on four sides surrounding an outdoor recreation area in the center. Outside of the few restrictions that electricity and plumbing impose, there are no rules. The house becomes a symbol of the family, a physical extension of members of the family.

THE HOLMES REVIEW

Occasionally a writer will get a chance to respond to a challenge similar to the one Ann Holmes found herself faced with. The fine arts editor of the *Houston Chronicle*, Ann is a critic with impeccable credentials. Hers is a respected voice in Houston, and she is a regular participant in national critical affairs. In the summer of 1987 she was elected co-chairman of the American Theater Critics Association, reflecting the respect she has in just one area of artistic evaluation. Architecture may not be her favorite art, but it is near the top, perhaps because she has more than a passing acquaintance with architect Philip Johnson, one of the century's great architects and ingenious innovators.

Johnson and his partner John Burgee were already well-known for their imaginative designs for Pennzoil Place in Houston and the striking AT&T building in Manhattan. It became known in Houston, via the business pages, that the famed team was working on a design for a new RepublicBank Center in the city's rapidly changing downtown area. It was to be a major building in the vicinity of 50 stories, the advance stories announced. Then came the formal revelation of the design, perhaps every bit as striking as the other structures these men have come to be known by. The plan was revealed with no accompanying information as to the source of the idea.

Ann took one look and saw something very familiar. "It's a guild house," she thought, and once back at the office consulted an old art history book she had had around since college days. Then she called her friend and said "Philip, you've designed a guild house, haven't you?" And he was delighted at her knowledge, but not surprised (personal communication, July, 1983).

The next step was to develop a full-length piece for the upcoming Sunday edition, and for this Ann delved into the background of guild halls, added information about the new building itself, and presented her readers with a fine lesson in modern design.[1]

A FUTURE WITH A PAST

By Ann Holmes
Fine Arts Editor

The flamboyant Serge Diaghilev was given to shouting at his artists "Astonish me." Few today are the artists who can really disarm, or astonish us, but one of them is architect Philip Johnson.

---

[1]Courtesy of the Houston *Chronicle*, June 21, 1981.

He did it with his Pennzoil Building, then again with the explosively controversial AT&T Building in New York with its broken pediment as a topknot, sort of a block off the old Chippendale. Then there was the huge glass Cathedral, for the drive-in church in Los Angeles.

We have seen his designs for the glass-gone-Gothic turreted building for Pittsburgh Plate Glass.

But with the announcement made last week by developer Gerald D. Hines Interests, the new RepublicBank Center will open some disbelieving eyes. Designed by Johnson and his partner John Burgee of New York, this new structure to occupy the block immediately west of their Pennzoil towers is bound to be the latest Johnson shocker. It must be said, however, that architecture watchers are becoming less surprised by new plans from this highly innovative firm which is reveling in the richness of historical heritage.

Their RepublicBank Center introduces the 17th-century Renaissance of the Netherlands into the multi-styled cacophony of midtown 20th-century Houston.

In a way it's a Dutch treat. The new design suggests the great old guild houses with their stepped gables that lined the plazas of Dutch, Flemish and north German towns. The Grand Plaza in Brussels built after the seige of 1695 is the last of the public squares surrounded by guild houses which were once found in all Flemish towns.

The Meat Hall in Haarlem, built by Lieven de Key in 1602-3, is another building admired for its stepped facade. And like it, Johnson/Burgee's RepublicBank Center has decorative finials.

The Rathaus or City Hall of Rothenburg, built in 1571 by Jakob Wolfe, and the Bremen Town Hall of 1609 both show Dutch influences in their massive buildings with the stepped gables. Some of these are more ornate than others, some show Gothic influences in asymetrical placement of doors or stairs, for instance.

There is a great deal of variety and evidence of overlapping influences in these earlier Renaissance buildings, which gives Johnson/Burgee a license they have taken.

Almost all tourists know the remnants of guild houses. They can also be seen in architectural tomes, and more excitingly in museums. Flemish artists painted townscapes that gave us handsome documentation of these buildings. One of these is Vermeer's The Street to Delft, in which the building in the forefront features a Vermeer woman in typical headgear sitting in a doorway sewing.

Houston's new RepublicBank Center distills the essence of these characterful buildings. There is the sense of pyramidal mass, the stepped roofline, and the finials that celebrate the verticality. These obelisks were added to "give a sparkling effect against the sky," Johnson said. This hasn't been seen in new construction in America since the Woolworth building was erected 70 years ago in New York.

Johnson and Burgee have taken the idea of this Renaissance scheme and have filtered it through their own contemporary wit and wisdom. They have produced a granite building that takes its place with 20th-century bravado in a square that already has medieval references—in the Alley Theater's turreted design by New York architect Ulrich Franzen.

"This wasn't our first idea," Johnson said. "We came up with several earlier designs. Not a one of them was like this. They were all glass."

Had they been harboring such an idea as the guild house for awhile?

"Absolutely not," swears Johnson. "It's brand new—a recent love."

Given the plan to work in stone and to answer their own sloped-roof Pennzoil project, Burgee said "the only way to end a stone building is with stepped roofs."

Johnson and Burgee had several unusual problems and certain advantages in designing this building. "It's hard to build a small building in the shadow of a big one," Johnson said. And though 56 stories is taller than Pennzoil Plaza, at 36 stories, the new bank had to make itself not only a compatible neighbor in design elements, but it had to become an equal, but not greater, architectural entity.

Moreover, it had to manage not to blanket the Pennzoil Building.

As the city's prime architectural logo, visible from Allen and Memorial parkways and the freeways that circle the city, Pennzoil deserves a certain protection. If anyone was to blanket it, who should do it with more delicacy and style than Johnson/Burgee themselves? Hines, a master at the choreography of architectural assignment, worked that out.

The problems were solved by creating a ground-level excitement as the grand entry of RepublicBank opens an almost chatty dialogue across the street with the western entry of Pennzoil. Like Dutch wives across a street, they've been sweeping. And the upper body of red granite—not unlike the red brick of the old Dutch buildings—very ably adds its own excitement to the city's many aerial configurations. That flame-finished, Napoleon-red granite color should add a new and animating hue to the desert tan, banker gray, corporate khaki and Dunhill-lighter green tones in which our skyscrapers have lately been ordered up.

The new bank center should become a midtown crossroads, as one can enter the new building from all four sides and move through a cruciform set of corridors inside, making the building answerable to all cardinal points, as well as to the extensive underground tunnel system.

In the upper building, the architects have created three separate stepped gables, a device which opens up the view to the Pennzoil from the freeways and provides the Pennzoil some tenants with a continuing view to the bayous and surrounding greenery—if they're up high enough.

Design-wise, this plan niftily responds in a refreshingly different tonality to Pennzoil's sloping glass roofs. But what's so pleasing to imagine is the aspect we should have from the Alley Theater, looking south. With the banking room side by side to the tower, and its staggered setbacks, the look should be that of guild houses, cheek by jowl, but with some of them grown Texas tall.

While its tower does not copy, it does take its germ of an idea from the dramatic contours of these Renaissance row houses. Sloping roofs in guild houses usually sported dormer windows. That at least we do not have. The stepped slopes nicely reflect a Gothic idea that is already familiar to the city in the terraced levels of the Gulf Building, though the steps there encircle the entire shaft.

Best of all, while the ceremonial entry is on Louisiana, the building presents its row house look to the Civic Center Plaza, which is historically appropriate. The banking room's 75-foot arched entryway could well be a dramatization of the arched entrance to de Key's famed Old Meat Market in Haarlem, Holland. So that R inevitably means Renaissance as well as RepublicBank.

A fascinating fact about the design is the selection of the banking room as a separate grade-level entity. Though it is a small version of the larger building at the sidewalk level, it is actually a stunning space that soars 12 stories, with a series of banked skylights that run the full 250-foot length of the building. The two buildings, side by side, one small, the other soaring to 56 stories, play games with your perception. One senses the banking room is a miniature when actually it is a giant. This is in keeping with Johnson's earlier famous experiment in scale: the Pavilion at his own estate in New Canaan, a diversion for those visiting the famous Glass House.

Certain Gothic paintings also employed the idea of strange perspectives in which the figures of full-sized people appeared in the foreground of religious works.

In all these ways, Johnson and Burgee have given Houston a richly faceted design to anticipate with relish. It is a startling new neighbor, all right, but it comes complete with good manners, not hogging the skyline, adjusting its own ebullient personality to the constraints of neighborhood design, and bringing its own fine cultural credentials with it.

One of the splendid things about this brilliant new silhouette is that it gobbles up the hideous little Western Union building (it will be encased inside) and becomes the city's own super-sized Gablegram.

Ann Holmes' review, which is as much a scholarly evaluation as a report, appeared in the Chronicle 5 days after the announcement of the new design. In those 5 days (more likely 3, given the early deadlines in special Sunday sections) she did enough homework and gave the matter enough thought to compare the new bank building to its European ancestors, to compare this design with earlier Johnson–Burgee schemes, and finally to project how it would look upon completion among its neighbors.

This is really more of a scholarly criticism than a review; the fact that it appeared so soon after the unveiling of the new building is a tribute to the writer's ability and training.

Most architecture reviews are more summary-report-feature stories than critical analyses. Almost every other kind of artistic expression stands the chance of having its success affected by the reviews; it is unlikely that a building was ever canceled as a result of an unfavorable notice. Additionally, the review is based on drawings and models, and in no other art is there such a passage of time between publication of the conception and completion.

THE SAME FORMULA APPLIES

If the reviewer does get a chance to write about a building, public or private, or a home, he should apply the same formula he follows in other arts, but treat it as one of the less familiar arts. The opening statement should be easy, because there will probably be a photograph involved. Identification consists normally of the name of the building, the architect, the location, and the tenant.

In the event the architect is well-known his or her other designs, or at least some of them, should be in the review. The building materials and colors can be included, as well as the general contractor, although that is more of a business page item. Similarly, the cost of the structure can be part of the review, or can be left for other parts of the newspaper. If the design is for a private home the review can only be written with the cooperation of the owners, and they may be unwilling to discuss cost.

Summary is almost all description, and the problem will be in limiting things to describe, although some discussion of the proposed function should be included. Fitting in with both identification and summary should be a building schedule, so readers of the review can know when to begin looking.

An interesting part of many architecture reviews of new downtown buildings is a description of what the land was used for before. Often a venerable old structure is razed to make way for a new building.

Opinion is probably the most difficult aspect to deal with, but luckily is almost unnecessary. The success of a design is determined in large part by how well it functions, and that is all but impossible to measure until the building is complete. As he points out the distinctive aspects of a plan, the writer is giving the public something to think about, and various members of the public may choose to be critical. This was certainly the case with the AT&T Building in New York with its striking pediment, and the John Hancock Building in Chicago, where the exterior placement of structural beams gives the giant building a gift-wrapped appearance.

In fact, every innovation in architecture, including the Empire State Building, has met with a fair share of negative comment. Yet the buildings still stand.

Chapter Ten
"It's Pretty, But is it Art?"

"I don't know anything about Art, but I know what I like."

What an incredible admission!

Critics, as a rule, write for an enlightened audience, and are not concerned with this familiar but ignorant position. But this is an attitude the reviewer must understand. The average person, who thinks he or she has an appreciation for art, will see no reason to study it or spend time analyzing it.

The writer must develop the ability to offer intelligent, even informed opinion about a piece of art even though he himself is anything but an expert. He does this by taking time to examine the medium.

A distinction that separates the fine from the performing arts is that they primarily represent the efforts of one person. By the time the general public is exposed to music, dance, and drama, many other parties have become involved, so that a performance represents the work of many, even though the original creativity came from one person.

With art, sculpture, and literature there is one artist, one creator, and among them, those who paint seem to be the most flamboyant, outrageous, and newsworthy. One tends to think of the likes of Picasso, Salvador Dali, Toulouse-Lautrec, Gaugin, Christo, and Andy Warhol. Norman Rockwell (actually an illustrator) seems unusual in that he appeared to be so normal.

KEEP THE EMPHASIS ON THE ART

The reviewer must keep in mind that he is writing about art, not the artist, or the artist primarily and incidentally his art. The trouble comes when the writer, meaning to comment on art, spends too much time and too much opinion on the artist. It would be unpopular as well as unwise to write about the works of a Dali or a

Warhol with only the briefest mention of the artist; readers would expect more. But it would be inappropriate to go on at great lengths about the personality or eccentricities of an artist not very well-known.

In terms of the actual review, summary in art, as in all the fine arts, is fairly simple, and is closely linked with identification; that is, complete identification indicating artist or artists, place and hours of exhibition, plus the number of works, when they were accomplished and what they consist of, would take care of both requirements.

The review could include a description of the material on exhibit; a painting, or six paintings, or a retrospective of more than 100 early and late works. If the exhibit represents more than one artist, that is part of the identification and the summary. But opinion, not surprisingly, is anything but simple.

Should newspaper editors and readers expect really intelligent criticism or merely description in entertainment writing that deals with art? Even the contemporary expert—the critic with years of training and appreciation—is hard-pressed to disagree with those who have already consigned Cezanne, Degas, Leonardo, and others to the area of the immortals.

The local reviewer may lack the credentials and the critical ability to pronounce a new work by a local semi-professional artist great, but he must still offer some opinion. If nothing else, he can say that a work is pleasing, contains a nice grouping of colors, conveys an interesting mood, has good brush work, was widely appreciated at the recent showing, has attracted offers at reasonable prices, or is generally an attractive work. Even if the work is an accepted masterpiece, he still has a responsibility to say why.

AN EXHIBIT IN COLORADO

Boulder, Colorado, has supported art for many years, and the local newspaper's coverage reflects this. When the annual all-media exhibit opened, the *Daily Camera* called on a recognized artist and critic to offer commentary. This review, typical of many that appear in newspapers away from the few huge art centers in the nation, combines opinion, description, and explanation. It has a strong opening statement, giving a clear indication of the tone of the review, and notice also how this writer handles summary.

She indicates that there are some 60 entries selected from many, then concentrates on those she feels are most noteworthy or representative. The reference in the eighth paragraph to the magazine cover is because the entertainment editor featured this review in the Sunday magazine section, and illustrated it with this work.[1]

THE JURY IS IN: ARTS '84 BLENDS THE RIGHT STYLES

By Jane Fudge
For the *Camera*

"This," as Ed Sullivan impressionists say, grimacing and twisting themselves up like pretzels, "is a really big shew."

---

[1]Courtesy of the Boulder, CO *Daily Camera*, March 23, 1984.

Arts '84 opens this evening at the Boulder Center for the Visual Arts. Though it lacks the amenities of the Beatles and poodles in ballet skirts, it has the proper variety and depth required of such exhibitions. On the whole, Lewis Story, interim director of the Denver Art Museum, and William Peterson, editor of Artspace Magazine in Alberquerque, have done a good job of winnowing several hundred entries down to the sixty-odd works in the galleries.

A juried show is a unique brew of the jurors' experience and prejudices and what the artists have on hand. The hemlines of art regularly go up and come down again, and any good juried show is a barometer of such changes.

Arts '84 is no exception, and while it is billed as an all-media exhibition, it is heavily weighted with paintings. After years of the hegemony of abstractionism, this show is mostly representaional. The hallmark of Arts '84 has to be the amazing recrudescence of figure painting.

The show is just the right size for the BCVA spaces; the largest works find sufficient elbow room in the West Gallery. The level of professionalism is high as well. It is good to see a number of fresh faces, both young artists and newcomers, though I had the impression that many long-established painters, especially in the Denver–Boulder area, had been drained off this year by the invitational "Colorado Painting Show" which opens at the Arvada Center next week.

Still-life painting seems a neglected area, but two of its practitioners are among Arts '84's best. Susan Cooper shows a handsome pastel of two self-luminous eggplants shimmering on a window ledge, exuding multicolored Kirlian auras. Cooper's violent palette and decorative instincts are balanced by some droll humor and quirky drawing, seen here in the fat moon that resembles the melon-slice crescents in Krazy Kat cartoons.

A row of small prints by Robert Ecker combine the intimacy of book illustrations and the surreal metaphysics of Rene Magritte. "This Is Not Cereal" naturally relies on its affinity with Magritte's famous semantic pipe, but it is also a sincerely wrought image of transcendence before breakfast, the unexpected experience of grace that pervades the short stories of Flannery O'Connor.

"Action #1," a picture of a paintbrush entombed beneath an epitaph of gestural painting, is likewise a reference to Magritte's "The Bold Sleeper" and a comment on the silly rhetorical question, "Is painting dead?"

Arts '84 encompasses a remarkably wide range of painting styles, from the harsh, funny punkamentaries of Zoa Ace to the suave abstract paintings of Richard Carter and Dave Yust.

Paul Gillis examines the artist's lot in "It Is the Same for ALL" (on the magazine cover) and finds a very nutty brand of creative anguish. An automation painter, rendered in Gillis' flat, precise style, is coming apart at the seams, gesturing rudely to his audience, then disintegrating into a red Rorschach soul and a clattering skeleton. Gillis is best known for his paintings of abstract sexual activities among mechanical forms. When he chooses more literal representation as he does here, the effect is both hilarious and profoundly distressing.

I was greatly impressed by an oil painting, "We're in the Grass, Now," by Jill Englebardt. Each time I looked at it, I discovered something more. That is a rare and rewarding happening at art shows. A reclining figure is half-obscured (or half-consumed) by a bonfire on a fleshy-looking lawn. A red fish and a shooting star bask in the light of the same weird satellite that enchants Susan Cooper's eggplants. Englebardt's painting is haunting without being self-consciously strange, and her color is rich even in passages with very narrow value contrasts.

In spite of its jarring color, there is something lonely about the empty garden bench in "Orange Pavilion Shadows" by Carolyn Reid. Her handling of paint is frankly derivative of the Post-Impressionists, and her color is about as hot and unnatural as it comes: enough cadmium red and yellow to paint a billboard ad for pizza. It is a startling work, and one that looks better and better with every pass.

Rayda Oakley paints over-life-sized portraits in a modest and restrained realistic style. She treats the still-life elements in her paintings with the same respect as her quintessentially middle-class sitters in "It's a Pretty Good Life." Her drawing is not as wiry as it might be for this kind of work, and I could not figure out the light source in this painting at all. That muddles its sturdy realism a bit, but on the whole it's a pretty good painting.

Other artists' techniques support their imagery less successfully.

Max Krimmel's amusing still-life "Oversize Stacks" depicts a library shelf presumably filled with the artist's favorites and presided over by a collection of wind-up toys. His painting style is dry and uningratiating, and the visual structure of the work is weak, though the idea carries well enough. (But does the spine of any art book really read "Jacques Villion?") The chilly eroticism of Irene Delka's big nudes would be far more convincing if the figures themselves were painted with the more relaxed technique she saves for their surroundings.

Abstract painters are outnumbered in Arts '84, but most hold their own. "Jetty Locker IV" by Richard Carter and "Geomantic Inclusion. Cool/Warm" by Dave Yust share landscape references and elegant color. These paintings are made with great confidence and accomplishment, though they are a little slick. Such cool and reposeful works, along with Gene Mathews' shimmering "Synth," are a welcome respite from the storm of figuration.

The landscape is represented realistically as well, notably by Bruce Cody in "House by an Overpass," and Jim Colbert's panoramic "Arizona Landscape." John Shively's "No Parking in Front of My House," is a kind of still-life landscape, if that is possible, with homage to Audrey Flack and others. It is very lusciously painted, but why, oh why did the artist stick all those plastic loops on the frame? I suppose they were intended to echo the contours of the painted objects. They look like mattress handles and are a gimmicky distraction from a good-looking work.

Lynn Grimes also weakens her glowing semi-abstract landscape "Desert Spaces, Comanche Gap" with an arty meteor shower of gestures. Both she and Shively are good painters; they just need to leave well enough alone.

There is only a smattering of photography in the show, and much of it is ordinary. Gary Emrich's TV images on sensitized Arches paper are conceptually ineresting and visually banal, which is just how they're supposed to be, I guess. The conventional prints are not great shakes, with the strong exceptions of Lynn Lickteig's Ophelia-like "Figure in a Landscape" and Lou Marcus' somber documentary silver print, "The Visit."

Three-dimensional works also run the gamut of styles and materials. Laura Thorne's brightly enameled metal sculpture is small, with an airy, graphic quality, yet it has all the spatial complexity of the artist's larger works. A large terra-cotta pot by Kathleen Smith-Schooley sports some wonderful glaze decoration on its elaborately contoured flanks. The obliquely sliced glass bowl by John Nickerson is fine looking, but his large glass vessel with fittings of polished aluminum is exquisite in its simplicity.

I visited the exhibition too early to see Diane Sandusky's "If I Had Been Born a Man" installed. Judging by other works by this sculptor, the work should be both visually exciting and provocative.

★ ★ ★

Jane Fudge is an artist, an art critic for several regional publications and a contributing editor to Artspace magazine.

Obviously, this writer has experience and credentials that surpass those of the average reviewer—for one thing, she uses the first person pronoun, a device normally left to the critic or extremely experienced and widely known reviewer—yet her report satisfies the conditions of a review. In particular, this is a good example of how to deal with less than satisfactory work. The review commends some artists, suggests what is lacking in others, and touches not only on many of the works, but on the show as a whole. In spite of the particular knowledge she brings to her writing, Jane Fudge's piece still serves as a model for those charged with covering an entire exhibit.

OPINION WITHOUT PRESUMPTION

The average writer's opinion is valuable and even necessary, but to protect himself from readers and editors alike, he must not act as if his is the final word. After a painting has stood the test of time, has been viewed by a large number of people including critics and experts, has been commended by other painters, and has been displayed at leading galleries, then it can be called successful, or good, or representative.

It would seem that truly great art, even moderately successful art, is judged by bulk, rather than individual, opinion. If this is, as it seems to be, a fact of life in the world of art, the reviewer's task becomes easier. He need not worry about calling something good or bad or mediocre at first glance, because his is not the final word. His voice is at best the first of many that will be raised in support of or against the work of art.

There might seem to be more reasons for the nonexpert not to offer opinions on art than reasons why he should pass judgment. Yet opinion must be present for the writing to be legitimately a review and not simply a news story. The newer at this assignment he is, the more time the entertainment writer should spend on description, rather than opinion.

Art by definition is a two-dimensional representation of an object, wherein some type of medium is applied in some manner to some type of surface, in what should be a pleasing, or satisfying, manner. It is called two-dimensional as a matter of convenience to distinguish it from sculpture. There are those artists who, using a pallette knife, spread their oils on canvas so thick that a three-dimensional effect is achieved. Others fashion deep frames that add a new dimension, and the collage makers frequently capitalize on the different weight and texture of materials they use. Art is normally portable, and is designed to give satisfaction to those creating, purchasing, and displaying it. Considering that art can involve any medium that can be put on a surface in some manner, the possibilities are indeed endless.

SURFACE, MEDIUM, AND APPLICATION

Now the variables enter, including the surface upon which the art appears—paper, canvas, walls, ceilings, wood, bricks, the inside of an eggshell; there is the medium—the paint or crayon or charcoal or pencil; and last, the method of application—brush, fingers, feet, roller skates. And this is only the beginning.

Modernist Andy Warhol blew up a panel from a comic strip and called it art. Pop artist Christo wrapped pink plastic around Florida islands and called it art. In the 1970s there was a fad based on spontaneity, where people created ''happenings'' by getting together, doing things, and calling it art. A beachcomber finds a piece of driftwood, a local craftsman builds a frame for it, and it is called art. Another glues a seashell to a piece of canvas and calls it art. An animal trainer turns loose a chimpanzee with paint and brush and canvas and calls it art.

As a promotional device to raise funds for the 1984 Olympic Games, stars of past Olympics used their athletic tools to create art. Basketball star Bill Russell dribbled a ball over a huge canvas, and hockey great Mike Eruzione used a hockey puck and stick to smear paint on another canvas. This was clearly a gimmick, and certainly the Olympic Committee made no pretensions about great creativity. Yet the probability is that many who purchased prints of the flurry of colors spread around a canvas refer to it as art.

A modern artist pastes strips of paper on canvas and calls it art. A painter pours paint from buckets onto canvas held at an angle, so the paint runs off, and calls it art. An entrepreneur hires a model in a bikini, places her on the floor, pours paint on the floor and tells her to roll around. A man sits on a low stool, 10 feet from his canvas and hurls globs of paint at it. The result, we are told, is art.

An old and outmoded theory is that if it is truly art, the creator should be able to go into another room and duplicate the thing exactly. This contention really does not hold up. Singers and actors do not give identical performances every time they take the stage, and even poets and authors would have trouble recreating exactly a poem of any length or a short story, once away from the typewriter.

The critic and her readers may be genuinely concerned about what is and what is not art. But the reviewer is writing for a wider audience, and to these readers, if the result of the application of paint to surface, in whatever manner, is pleasing, if it satisfies the owner or the viewer, then it hardly seems right to quibble about whether it is indeed true art. To many people, novelty is as much an attribute as creativity.

A DEFINITION ISN'T EASY

Does this mean, then, that art is anything one wishes it to be? Is this creative anarchy? This is a step beyond the concept that there is beauty in everything into the area where any activity that includes some kind of material can be termed artistic. Some people talk about artistry in cake decorating, in table setting, in landscaping; there are talented cooks, genius bookkeepers, gifted house painters. Some would say that this is getting absurd, but then where is the line drawn?

Surely the schooled artist, familiar with traditional media and trained by accepted mentors who produces a pleasant landscape has given us art. But when a madman locks himself in a completely dark room and by feel and inspiration scribbles on a wall, is it art or novelty? Creation or accident?

In the 1980s there was a recurring interest in the art of Adolph Hitler, spawned probably by the appearance of so-called Hitler diaries that were later found to be hoaxes. Still, there were any number of reports of paintings done by the madman of World War II selling for large sums, perhaps more money than was being attracted by the works of two other well-known contemporary amateurs, Winston Churchill and Dwight Eisenhower.

The distinction between art and novelty must be clear in the arts writer's mind. He must somehow define his own limitations or areas of interest, and follow that definition as he reports on art.

Much of what this typical reviewer is called on to analyze is amateur art at county fairs, at annual exhibitions presented by schools and colleges and universities, and displays of members' works by art clubs. These artists are all amateurs, usually taking lessons. Occasionally, one of the more talented will sell a painting, but that is not the goal. They are interested in art as a hobby, as a means of self-expression, or as a social activity, and this is how they should be regarded. Most will not have the skill or the courage to attempt portraits or even realistic landscapes, and many will limit themselves to what they might call modern art.

Developing an Opinion About Art

The writer should have some feeling for the concept, the tools, and the process that was followed to produce the work in question. Then he must have some method of developing an opinion, some standards on which to base his judgment. The first task is relatively easy, the second at times impossible, but without giving proper attention to each the entertainment writer is committing a most serious offense; he is not only doing injustice to an art form, he is also misleading his readers who look to him for guidance and instruction.

To begin with, the art is on something, canvas or paper or some other material, including metal. This is normally a part of basic identification and summary. It would not automatically apply in the case of a Cezanne retrospective, for example, a showing of a number of the artist's selected works covering a certain period of his life, because in that event the assumption would be clear that he was painting on canvas. Still, the painstaking writer will see that the phrase "oil on canvas" appears some place in his review. The description of surface is more important in new, unreviewed works.

The manner of applying paint or some other transferable material to the surface is next. Conventionally it is by brush, but a contemporary artist may use a pallette knife, hands, rags, or other tools. Still, simply saying "brushes" may not be enough. Renaissance masters who dealt in miniatures—tiny, marvelously intricate paintings in oil—would at times use a single hair to apply paint. Bristles or hair in brushes can be soft or firm, long or short, fine or dense and bushy. The writer examining an old master can see where the artist used one brush for rough-textured clothing, another for smooth flesh tones.

If it seems appropriate, the writer can discuss with the artist the method of application and the type of tools used, and this might provide a basis for evaluation. Unless the writer is something of an artist himself he may not realize the skill involved in producing the painting. Ignorance can be eased by asking the right questions of the artist, or another knowledgeable person.

The material to be applied could be oil, acrylic, water color, pencil, pen, charcoal, or strawberry jam. Each medium has different qualities and poses different problems, both in application and analysis. Oil tends to be thicker and permanent, pastels can be wonderfully suggesting, ink can be interesting, pencil challenging.

MOST FRAME THEIR OWN WORKS

Framing is a major concern of artists themselves. Most painters will insist on framing their own works, aware that balance between frame and painting is essential. The frame could be stained wood, unfinished wood, driftwood, seasoned wood, metal, rope, or other material. It should not detract from the painting; the painting is the star, the frame the support, and the correct balance should be retained. A poor job of framing or an inappropriate frame offers material for a negative opinion, just as the ingenius use of certain material for framing could be the reason for a more positive review. To ignore framing at an exhibition is the same as overlooking supporting roles at the theater.

Whether the piece of art being discussed is part of a permanent collection or on loan, it should be placed in such a way so that the viewer can see the artist's intent. If it has a glass cover, as do most watercolors, there should be no distracting reflections from lights. Even oils, if poorly lighted, can show blind spots, or areas of glare if the lighting is too direct or too strong. This is the museum or gallery director's responsibility, to display what he or she has to show to its best advantage.

The artist is not to blame when his or her works are poorly exhibited; an art exhibit could be reviewed positively in terms of the works involved, but negatively because of the way they were hung. The writer needs to ask himself if the lighting is adequate and appropriate, and if the paintings are too close together or too far away from each other. The director starts with a certain amount of floor and wall space, certain lighting capability, and a knowledge of the predictable traffic pattern through his halls. Skill, taste and care all go into the successful hanging of an exhibit.

The review that touches only on the quality of the works of art and ignores the staging is incomplete. If the writer feels inadequate to go much further he can still do a relatively good job, and provide a service to his readers, by limiting himself to a description of the exhibit in terms of works, media, staging, and such routine matters as hours of exhibition, a necessary part of identification, and a brief biography of the artists. Then it is not too difficult to begin injecting opinion, but it must be supported by example.

A Problem in Florida.   St. Petersburg, Florida, boasts of a marvelous collection of the works of the eccentric Salvador Dali, including some of the artist's giant canvases. Unfortunately, the lighting in the gallery is such that it is all but impossible to get a clear look at the works unimpeded by glare from the lights. This is partially because even though most of the works are in oil—and in most galleries oils are not covered—these Dali paintings are all under glass, and because of their size, pick up unwanted reflections from overhead lights.

Any writer can describe paintings in terms of being realistic, or abstract, but when it comes to describing art in terms of schools and styles, the program notes can be his best friend, as long as he uses them as a point of departure. The reviewer should read the technical explanation in the program, then translate it into acceptable newspaper prose for his readers.

The review will almost always contain something about the artist, what else he has done, and what acceptance this particular work or exhibit has had in other quarters, if it has been seen before. When a new painting is revisited, when galleries are asked to provide copies, when magazines and art experts praise it, when other galleries seek to borrow it for a showing, then does modern, or new art, become established and accepted.

TWO AREAS OF ACCOMPLISHMENT

A discussion of art and the reviewer's responsibility should include two areas of considerable artistic accomplishment—illustration and photography.

Illustrators

An illustrator, be he a Norman Rockwell or a Currier and Ives, is not the same as an artist, even though his skill may be equal or even greater. An illustrator provides a representational image of a story or theme or person designed to enhance or augment the story or, as in the case of Rockwell's famous *Saturday Evening Post* covers, to convey a general mood or feeling.

Certainly there is a tremendous amount of creativity, talent, and ingenuity in advertising art, but it is primarily illustration, where the motivation is to call attention to a product or a story, rather than to let the illustration stand by itself. Just as obviously there are illustrators who have created genuine art.

The Strange Frenchman Was an Exception

Toulouse-Lautrec, the odd but interesting Frenchman who is perhaps best known for his posters depicting action in Parisian cabarets, was an illustrator who was also an artist. He was also so gifted, the experts believe, that his illustrations are generally regarded as art. Norman Rockwell did some work that was not purely illustrative, and he was certainly a skilled and accomplished craftsman, but the bulk of his work, and the work he is best known for, is in the category of illustration, and that is why he is an illustrator. Perhaps 100 years from now history will have consigned him to a higher category, perhaps not. The categories of artist and illustrator are not mutually exclusive

Photographers

It may not be too many years before photography deserves a chapter by itself. Photography has been gaining steadily as an activity that produces art. Photographs taken by students of the University of Houston's brilliant Fred Baldwin appear in movie houses throughout the nation between showings of feature films.

In North Dakota, a public television station has taken advantage of interested photographers to produce background shots for station identification. Janna Anderson, whose primary interest is in the fine and performing arts, saw this as a chance to expand her subject area, and wrote about it for her newspaper's Sunday Travel and Arts section. Her account is part interview, part announcement, and part review.[2]

PPTV EXHIBITION FOCUSES ON OUR WORLD

By Janna Q. Anderson
Entertainment Editor

Classy yet folksy. Artsy yet down-home. Real. They may be on-screen for only seconds, but they grab your attention instantly with a simple statement that says more than the embossed words "Prairie Public Television."

They're the photographs used during the station breaks on the area's public television stations, and they're done so well they've made it to the big time—an art exhibition.

About 40 of the 2,200 images in Prairie Public Television's station identification slide collection have been printed, framed and put on view at the Rourke Gallery, 523

---

[2]Courtesy of the Fargo *Forum*, Fargo, ND—Moorhead, MN, September 18, 1983.

4th St. S., Moorhead. They're on display through Oct. 2, along with a videotape show of 600 of the slides. The entire show will later be sent out to tour the area.

The slides are simple images that reflect everyday life on the prairie and in our cities and small towns. They were aired beginning in 1981, the brainchild of PPTV art director Les Skoropat.

"We were expanding our library of I.D. slides, and I wanted a different slide for every break," he said. "Ross Rorvig (Rothsay, Minn.) and Deb Wallwork (Fargo) were among the first people to work at it. I told them I was looking for photos that were design-oriented and connected with this area."

That's what they came up with.

A number of different shooters, including Dianne Monson, Fargo; Brian Paulsen, Grand Forks, N.D.; Murray Lemley, Hope, N.D., and Scott Gunvaldson, Fergus Falls, Minn., have taken the pictures over the past couple of years. Sometimes they've been paid for their work, but most of it has been on a volunteer basis. Skoropat gives them color slide film, and they go out taking pictures.

"Prairie Public Television covers one of the largest geographic areas of any television operation in North America," Skoropat said. "Since our signal reaches from Fargo, North Dakota, all the way to North Battleford, Saskatchewan, we felt our I.D. project should represent the entire area . . . the pace of life, the agriculture, the people, recreation and the natural beauty of the prairie."

Federal regulations require that television stations identify themselves to viewers at least once every hour. Most stations use slides, but they don't put this much time and effort into them. Not nearly as much.

"There is this wonderful subject matter all around us that people just don't see," Rorvig said. "The real challenge of photography is to make rather mundane subject matter seem interesting."

Wallwork agreed.

"I don't think people always understand photographers," she smiled. "I'd be in someone's back yard, just enraptured by their garden hose . . . and they'd probably look out and think, 'Oh, no. It's the CIA come to check out my petunias!' "

The 35mm slides are cropped to meet television's 3x4 proportions. They are also altered by TV's limited range of color, contrast and detail. The photographers have been learning to adjust their shooting style to take this into consideration.

"When we began this project, people were skeptical," said Skoropat. "They thought it was another of those crazy ideas from the art department. But I knew it was going to be a big project. I was watching the photographers' styles develop. It was exciting. I wanted to do something more with the photographs.

"We've gotten so many positive reactions to the slides from viewers. People even call wanting copies of them. I wanted to be able to show the photographs in a more permanent form than these eletronic images that are there and gone. That's how the idea for the art exhibit came about.

"People don't have to be in their living rooms watching their television sets to see them. They're in a gallery, framed and matted, and you can stand and look at them as long as you like."

According to Skoropat, the photo project has now halted temporarily.

"There is very little money in our budget right now, so small items like film and slide mounts are some of the first things to go when they're paring things down. We're investigating new sources of funding, but right now we're in kind of a holding pattern."

The exhibition is being funded by the North Dakota Council on the Arts; Knight Printing, Fargo; Azo Color Labs, New York; the Plains Art Museum; the North Dakota Art Gallery Association; and Prairie Public TV. The display will open Oct. 7 at Bismarck Junior College's Gannon Gallery.

"When people watch Prairie Public Television now, they'll look for the I.D. slides," said Wallwork.

This is a good example of how a writer can combine the elements of a review with a feature-interview. Even though Anderson felt perfectly at home with her subject, she could have used this same format to report on an area of creativity she had less familiarity with.

Photographers themselves are quick to point out that actually exposing the film is the easiest part of the process. They say that the purely mechanical function of photography, which keeps many purists from accepting it as art, is almost incidental to the finished product. Far more important are selecting the location, film, light and lens opening, then most important, the developing. The successful photo, the prize winner, is a combination of the photographer's patience in waiting for perfect lighting, if it is an outdoor shot, or making the perfect lighting arrangements if it is inside; then the correct shutter speed, the film itself, the kind of paper the print will appear on, and the patience and skill that go into developing.

In the final analysis, photography that is artistic, such as a carefully planned study of a sunrise, as opposed to representational, such as a typical news shot, is judged as art; not as a separate art, but as part of the larger category of two dimensional art.

Chapter Eleven

Sculpture—Thousands of Years of Art

Few among the young plan careers as sculptors.

One reason could be the material needed; once past modeling clay, sculpture requires a major investment in space, substance, and equipment. And, although experience in the other arts is usually part of a basic education, trying one's hand at sculpture is not.

Sculpture is not a common art, although it may well be the one most associate with antiquity. Few critics concentrate on sculpture; still, like architecture, when something worth writing about appears, the skills of critics and reviewers alike are much in demand.

Never in recent history was this brought out more dramatically than on Veterans Day of 1982, when a guilt-ridden nation dedicated a new and most controversial monument honoring the dead of the Vietnamese War.

AN UNUSUAL BEGINNING FOR A MEMORIAL

A grass roots committee, lead by a Vietnam veteran named Jan Scruggs, spearheaded the effort to establish a lasting memorial for the dead of that war. It was to be financed entirely through donations, with the government supplying the land. A competition was held for the design of the monument, and architects and sculptors alike entered by the hundreds.

Of the more than 1,400 entries, one haunted the committee, design 1,026. The committee selected it from some 39 finalists, then went back and re-examined its choice, and selected 1,026 again.

Only then did the selectors find out that 1,026 was the design of 20-year-old Maya Lin, who submitted the now famous chevron-shaped cutout as an architectural class assignment. The selection evoked both praise and outrage, so much so that a companion piece, a traditional sculpture by 38-year-old Frederick Hart, a widely known sculptor, was placed near the Lin design.

Often overlooked in recalling the outpouring of emotion that began that Veteran's Day in 1982, when the monument was dedicated, was that this was a blending of the arts.

The committee had insisted that all 58,000 names of those lost in the war be on the monument, and many felt the arrangement should be alphabetical. No, Lin argued, they should be listed in the order in which they died, so the wall would read like an epic Greek poem.

Practicality won out, because there were so many similar names—more than 600 Smiths, 16 James Joneses—that an observer said the monument would read like a telephone book.

The *National Geographic*[1] summed up the artists nicely: "The wall and statue would come from a woman too young to have experienced the war and a man who never served in the military and said he had been gassed in an antiwar demonstration."

The monument seeks to make no political statement, it serves only to honor the dead. Yet hardly a day goes by without some mention of the tremendous emotional impact the memorial has made.

SCULPTURE CAN BE ALMOST ANYTHING

Sculpture is three-dimensional, comes in a limitless variety of sizes and materials, and is, perhaps, the only art form that immediately conjures up 2000-year-old images. Basically it is either statuary, in classical terms meaning people, or relief, when the subject was an event. The layman can define this as being either free-standing and more or less complete (statuary), or attached to a larger block of material yet still three-dimensional (relief).

A newspaper could run a picture of the statue, and the review could say "Look, there it is." But the writer's task is to describe the object in his review, not to rely on pictures. The picture is only a flat illustration, and can not do justice to a three-dimensional object.

First of All, What Does it Look Like?

This three-dimensional object either looks like someone, a military leader, a statesman, a poet—or it suggests something, a figure, an animal. But even a non-representational object should also suggest a feeling—bulk, power, warmth, or grace. It is more important to describe the work than to place it into a certain category.

---

[1] *National Geographic, 167*(5), May, 1985.

The review should indicate if it is representational or not, and if there are recognizable figures, either realistic or stylized.

Sculpture is described in terms of size and physical dimensions. Some statuary is life size, some is larger-than-life, and can be called heroic, depending on the subject; some is three-quarter size, some is miniature, although that is not a word normally associated with sculpture. If the sculpture is realistic, general terms such as "life size" are good to use. If it is much smaller, refer to it as, for instance, "a grouping of three standing figures roughly three feet high." If width or depth is a factor, mention it. Readers are not automatically familiar with weight, so saying it is a ton-and-a-half work of art may be meaningless.

Depending on the material used, the weight can vary tremendously and is seldom a factor in a review. If some gigantic monolith has been moved intact from one continent to another the weight would be part of the story, but that would be more of a feature aspect than an artistic consideration.

The name of the work should be accompanied or closely followed by a general description of the type of statue. A realistic piece called "Mother and Child" could show the clearly definable shape of a woman holding an infant. Another work could similarly be called "Mother and Child," but could consist of two large pieces of material, one about twice the size of the other, connected by a frayed piece of rope. Sculpture is more often than not what the sculptor says it is. In abstract art it is important to know what the artist had in mind, and his or her title is a valuable clue. Of course when he or she titles it "Work—1981," and it seems to have no recognizable shape—that is, it is in no way representational—the writer loses that edge.

Sculpture Is Judged by Location

Surroundings are important, regardless of where the sculpture is displayed. It might be indoors, discreetly placed in a dimly lit corridor between show rooms in a gallery; or spotlighted immediately inside the main doors; or even centered alone in a small, brilliantly lit room just off the main exhibition hall. The writer reports if it is in a permanent or temporary setting, if it is on loan and placed in an area obviously not designed for sculpture, and if it is outdoors, whether the exhibitor had any control over the location. These are basic components of identification and summary.

Opinion is not going to be as clearly pronounced in most reviews of sculpture for the same reasons that it is not a major factor in architecture. In today's world, sculpture is approved, commissioned and paid for on the basis of scale models or drawings, so the moment a sculpture actually appears it has already earned some approval. And, as in architecture, an unfavorable review is unlikely to have any bearing on the future of the piece of art, although it could have an effect on the future of the artist.

A danger area for critics and reviewers alike is modern sculpture that often seems formless. Panels of steel, various three-dimensional shapes assembled and welded together, towering abstract figures—all tend to puzzle the onlooker accustomed to representational, or realistic art. Those commissioning an important sculpture who follow a contemporary path, look to the style of those artists generally accepted as being great—the Picassos, the Moores, the Miros; then they buy or order a piece, and as often as not the reaction is, at best, mixed. The press needs to remember that contemporary giants were innovators, and that only after a period of time were they deemed to be great masters.

Many universities and shopping and civic centers make good use of sculpture and water. These are permanent arrangements, and in reviewing them the writer considers surrounding buildings and streets and objects. Commissioned sculpture must be compatible with the architectural style of the building it graces, which presents a further demand on the artist and consideration for the reviewer.

Chicago has its controversial Picasso, and Houston has a large Miro, each in a busy downtown setting. An appreciation of either must take into account what is nearby—parking lots, sidewalks, buildings, signs, whether the mammoth sculpture is in turn dwarfed by towering buildings, or whether it seems to be in balance with its surroundings.

The larger the sculpture, the more important the setting; the effect of a large work, either indoors or out, is destroyed if the view of part of it is continually blocked by traffic, an open door, or some other form of disruption that the planners should have considered. It makes sense that relatively small, portable sculpture can be easily displayed, whereas the massive, voluminous, heavy, heroic pieces present problems.

A Lesson from the Past

The marvelous relics from King Tut's tomb that toured America with tremendous success in the late 1970s were familiar because of the many times they had been photographed. Yet a photograph is a two-dimensional representation, and those actually seeing the objects from the boy king's tomb were amazed at the beauty and the detail on the back, or reverse, or unphotographed side, of the pieces. The objects were displayed in glass cases, all sides were well lighted and easily visible, and the reviews invariably complimented those who had staged the exhibit. The writer needs to report how the sculpture is displayed, just as he needs to mention if there are cables or concrete bases or wooden supports or other means to make the sculpture more visible.

The argument has been made that the critic evaluating a new outside sculpture should study it at different times of day, during good and bad weather, and also at different times of year, to observe how the shifting of the sun's light changes its appearance. Although this is not practical, it does not mean that this aspect should be ignored. After a review appears, the reviewer does not then give up interest in the object.

If nothing else, the writer can use a second look at a piece of sculpture as an item in a column, or as part of an advance story for another exhibit. Just as regular columnists comment on the changing seasons, as leaves turn color then fall, only to reappear, so might the arts writer discuss a piece of outdoor sculpture that takes on a new feeling as the winter sun changes the pattern of shadows.

At some point in his review the writer needs to deal with material. There can be no complete list of materials available to the sculptor, because anything that can hold a shape can lend itself to three-dimensional forms. Tradition means bronze and stone, but tradition doesn't always pertain. Metal in all forms, wood, plastics, clay, even water can be the medium of choice.

ART IS WHERE YOU FIND IT

A lot of sculpture, some of it worth preserving, is made from what are called *found objects*. These include the refuse of the beach—shells and driftwood; objects found in junkyards—parts of old cars and machinery; and clothing and broken utensils. This can also be dangerous ground. Anyone can glue a sea shell to a piece of wood, or polish an old brake drum and suspend it from a wooden frame. The writer dealing with amateurs will find a lot of this.

Although it may be more in the category of novelty than art, this kind of activity should not be discouraged. It does provide an outlet for some interested people, and as long as nobody is charging an outrageous sum to look at it there is no real reason to denigrate it. It is best to revert to basic journalism and write a report, rather than a review, about such examples.

On the other hand, there are those who have ground and polished beach glass, have sanded and stained driftwood, and have indeed produced attractive, artistic objects. But in those cases something was done with the material, and there is evidence of creative thought and skill and artistry.

The writer will have difficulty in describing the material and the method of construction of a piece of sculpture if it is not obvious, such as hewn or carved wood, or chiseled stone. Most readers will know that statues of bronze are cast from molds built on a clay model, but this may need to be explained, just as the writer should indicate how many bronze castings were made before the mold was destroyed. This information should come from either the artist or the agency or gallery in charge of the piece.

There is no magic number that determines how many models of a statue there can be before art becomes mass production, but obviously the fewer there are, the rarer and more valuable the statue. In sculpture and in reproduced paintings, the earlier the copy the cleaner the lines, and also, the earlier the copy, the more valuable it is. With some of the more modern and less familiar materials, the writer needs to rely on catalogs and brochures.

What can be of more general interest, and a part of the review, is a description of the tools used to create the work. Early sculptors used hammers and chisels, working in stone, or their hands, if the medium was clay; and one can only marvel at the patience it took Michelangelo to carve out his David. The modern sculptor working in the classical medium would have access to jackhammers, hydraulic lifts, and power tools, including sanders, and even elaborate equipment to test the density of his medium. The great Michelangelo got by on hands and heart.

MODERN ARTISTS, MODERN TECHNIQUES

The Snelson Exhibit

Typical of many successful modern sculptors is the engineer-turned-artist Kenneth Snelson, who works with steel and aluminum tubes and cable, and creates geometric, three-dimensional structures that are at least mechanically intriguing, and, at best, genuinely interesting pieces of art.

A typical Snelson exhibit consists of written plans for the pieces, and scale models, perhaps 1 or 2 feet in height or length, next to the finished sculpture. This exhibits not only the end result of the artist's creativity, but the steps along the way. And in the case of this man, his engineering background is apparent and unique. To review Snelson without commenting on his training would be to write an incomplete review.

He is one of those who number among the sculptor's tools blowtorches and welding irons. In such cases it is a good idea to give a description of the sculptor's studio, even though it is not likely to be a first hand account. Of more importance, though, would be a discussion of the sketches, drawings and models that were accomplished in advance of the actual sculpture. As is the case with Snelson, such material usually accompanies the works in the exhibit.

Here is how the *Buffalo News* dealt with a Snelson exhibit. Anthony Bannon, who wrote the advance, is the full-time art critic for the newspaper. Jack Foran, who did the review, is a frequent contributor.[2]

SNELSON AT THE ALBRIGHT-KNOX

Wired tight for perfection, the sculpture of Kenneth Snelson commands an heroic appreciation rare amid late 20th century cynicism, when heroes are few and ideals lost to life's struggles. For many, though, Snelson is a hero—like Picasso in an earlier age, or Buckminster Fuller more recently. With many, mention of the coming Snelson exhibition at the Albright-Knox Art Gallery draws an enthusiasm usually reserved for championship sports or more private passions such as weekly poker games, garage sales and disco dancing.

During the next week, the back lawn of the Albright will be busy with the construction of Snelson's giant wire strung polished metal tubes, anticipating a gallery members opening Friday evening, followed by a public opening Saturday. More than 30 of his smaller works will be installed in the Albright's Temporary Exhibition rooms, as well, with several of his drawings, models and panoramic photographs.

Organized by Albright Chief Curator Douglas G. Schultz, this first retrospective

---

[2]Courtesy of the Buffalo *Evening News*, September 6, 18, 1981.

for the popular American artist just completed an enthusiastic exhibition in the Hirsh-horn Museum in Washington. It will travel upon completion here Nov. 8 to the Sarah Campbell Blaffer Gallery at the University of Houston.

Snelson's work has enjoyed commissions in numerous public spaces in the United States, including Chicago, Baltimore, Washington and, last year, Buffalo. Like the technological elegance of a suspension bridge, Snelson's sculpture supports itself in aesthetic demonstration of the conceptual perfections of mathematics and philosophy. Its polished, mirror-like surfaces capturing and reflecting light, the work becomes a paradigm of idealism, light-struck and magical, just the right model for a struggling, re-building city. This was the most important fact that Buffalo's know-nothings ig-nored in their outcry against his sculpture after its installation on Niagara Square.

"The Romantic spirit of striving and becoming is apparent in Snelson's art," wrote Howard N. Fox of the Hirshhorn in his exhibition essay. Snelson's aspiration, he con-tinued, is nothing less than "to devise something immutable and perfect."
—Anthony Bannon

This shows that an advance can contain elements of other types of writing, in this case a commentary, with editorial overtones. The first notice appeared Sept. 6, and the review followed 12 days later.

SCULPTOR KENNETH SNELSON AND THE ARCHITECTURE OF THE ATOM

By Jack Foran
News Contributing Reviewer

Buffalo's fortunate to have a Kenneth Snelson tensegrity sculpture in Niagara Square, as also, currently, to have a retrospective exhibit of his works at the Albright-Knox Gallery.

All the work is beautiful and complex, intriguing, fascinating. Looking at it inspires wonder.

Where did the artist ever come up with such an idea—the tensegrity idea of separate, pipe-like pieces held together in equilibrium by a minimum network of cables, so that the pieces seem suspended in air? The beauty and fascination of the apparent free sus-pension is equaled by that of the actual perfect balance of physical forces.

How did he put the works together? He explains in a diagram included with a piece called "V—X."

People say the piece in Niagara Square doesn't go with the building it's in front of—City Court—or with Niagara Square in general. Why not? It contrasts with, and so compliments, just about everything else in the square.

But if it doesn't particularly do anything for the City Court building, so what? No sculpture or artwork is going to help that building, which is cold, impersonal, unintelligible—What's the plan of the building? How do you get into it? Where's the door?—Monumental, but a monument to nothing.

Buckminster Fuller, who invented the geodesic dome, coined the word "tensegri-ty" to describe Snelson's structural principle. Tension integrity. It's the same princi-ple as in Fuller's dome.

The breakthrough structural quality of the geodesic dome is that structural elements are in a tension balance. The gravitational weight of the dome is carried not just by anti-gravitational thrust, as in the traditional arch or dome, but each structural member is, as it were, self-supporting—part of a network equilibrium.

Snelson's art makes the geodesic situation visible.

But it does so only incidentally. Snelson's primary purpose is not to illustrate architecture, in the usual sense of buildings, but to illustrate the atom, the ultimate building block. The architecture of the atom.

The atom is his paradigm. If atoms exist as something other than mathematical equations, they're a matter of balance of forces, elements that are separate, yet bound together in an equilibrium of pushes and pulls.

Included in the exhibit is a series of verbal and drawing studies entitled: "Portrait of an Atom," subtitled: "A most didactic work of art," and dated 1960-80. It starts with the question: "Is the atom's electronic structure a reasonable subject for an artwork?" The answer: "Of course. Artists have often explored the invisible, the ghosts of the mind."

The artist's job is to make the invisible visible.

People say Snelson's work is technology, not art. What's the difference? Somebody makes something. If it's beautiful, we call it art. If it's useful, we call it technology. If it's both beautiful and useful, like the Verrazano Narrows Bridge or the Ellicott Square Building, it's obviously both art and technology.

The chief concern of both categories, moreover, is economy of means to a conceptual end.

The tensegrity sculptures are useful as illustrations and explorations of principles of structure. Part of the point is to show art and technology as a continuum.

Standing on the lawn of the Albright-Knox Art Gallery, you can observe the Snelson works set up there and at the same time the caryatids—the carved females functioning as pillars—on the small porches on the wall of the gallery.

The caryatids are copies from a Greek temple on the Acropolis. Whatever the original symbolism of the human figures as pillars, part of it, surely, was to express the felt vitality or dynamism of the support force of the pillars.

It's an allegorical representation, a primitive metaphor.

The tensegrity works express the dynamism directly, visibly in the structure itself.

The Snelson piece outside City Court is on permanent display. The exhibit at the Albright-Knox continues through Nov. 8.

The sculpture review should make it clear whether the writer saw the actual piece of sculpture, or a model, drawing, or photograph. Let the writer treat the announcement and accompanying sketches as a news story, then when the sculpture is complete, it can be reviewed as an artistic expression.

On another front, more and more universities and governmental bodies are specifying that funds for sculpture should be included in budgets for new buildings.

Much modern sculpture is commissioned, and the writer should find out the terms of the commission. Shopping centers and malls and public buildings stage competitions for sculpture to grace the finished center. Sculptors wishing to compete are told of certain restrictions, such as the general size of the sculpture, the size, coloring and shape of surrounding buildings, the suggested material, minimum and maximum dimensions, and other considerations such as including water, or benches where shoppers can sit. Competing sculptors create and submit models. The judges make their selection on the basis of the models, then commission the winner to produce the work. The writer can produce what appears to be a review, based on the competition and a study of the winning model. However, when it comes to expressing opinion, he is much better off quoting the reasons the judges gave for selecting the winner, rather than trying by himself to attach certain artistic qualities to it.

When it is complete there will be some kind of formal unveiling, and this is the appropriate time for the legitimate review and the writer's own opinion, based on what he can now see.

Many of today's artists hold academic positions with colleges and universities. It is helpful to know the terms of such a sculptor's employment, if he is required to exhibit, or only encouraged. Similarly, if the artist is not attached to a university, it becomes a matter of interest to know how he makes a living. If he is tremendously successful and supports himself entirely on commissions, that should be part of the story. Some teaching sculptors supplement their salaries by striking (designing) medals to commemorate important occasions. Often these are not as creative as the artist would like, because the general image and even the wording is assigned, but it is a good way to make some money.

Sculpture being what it is, there are not too many persons around who can claim it as a full time, financially successful occupation.

Chapter Twelve
Familiar Subject, Unusual Treatment

LITERATURE REVIEWS

Literature is one of the seven traditional arts, but the book review, unlike any of the others, gets its own peculiar treatment.

Book reviews are found in various places in the newspaper, most commonly collected in a Sunday edition book section. Book reviews might be the concern of an amusements, features, or fine arts staff, but regardless of their location they are the responsiblitiy of someone called the book editor. This person is more manager than reviewer. Book reviews, unlike any other area of comment on the arts, are produced by a large number of people, most of whom do not work for the newspaper.

Literature is an area of artistic expression where there are hundreds of books available, but each will attract a relatively small number of readers. Still, there must be someone on the staff who makes the decision about which books will and will not be reviewed. This determination, given the tremendous number of titles available, is often capricious.

The book editor on a smaller newspaper will normally try to get reviews of books on the *New York Times* or wire services best-seller lists, plus any new titles that members of the newspaper staff, or even a regular outside reviewer, might want to write about. The difficulty is that books appearing on a best-seller list have already been deemed to be of value, and have received considerable public acceptance. A local review may be not be much more than a repeat of what has already been written.

The book editor, if he wishes, can get a supply of ready-made reviews from publishers and syndicated news and feature services. They are safe comments and spare the local staff the task of deep thought. Another problem with best sellers is that many reviewers will simply rehash the material appearing on the jacket cover, and call it a review.

There Must Be a System

The book editor must develop some kind of system of selection, based on his time and resources and the amount of space he can count on. Then he must assemble a stable of reviewers, most coming from outside the newspaper, who he can trust to provide reasonably intelligent and accurate reviews. Large metropolitan newspapers can call on as many as 100 different readers to provide reviews, and in addition will frequently seek out specialists in a field to review new books in that area.

At the *Houston Post*, Eric Gerber moved up to book editor from film writer. A book section of a typical Sunday Arts and Entertainment section included the following reviewers: A syndicated reporter who writes about television, reviewing a book on political advertising on television; a local journalist who contributes to the *Post*'s Sunday magazine, writing about a new novel; an assistant news editor writing about an historical novel; Gerber himself, dealing with a book about a Japanese baseball star; another syndicated writer reviewing a book on the Kennedy family; a *Post* columnist dealing with a popular history of England; an official of the Texas Instutute of Letters, writing about a diary of a World War II flyer; and a librarian criticizing a new novel.

Gerber (personal communication, July, 1983) has found that the variety among reviewers as well as among titles is such that he can not produce a standard set of instructions for all. What instructions there are are on an individual basis depending on the particular book, the particular reviewer, and his needs at the moment (a lengthy analysis, or a short, breezy piece). With that in mind, he passes along these basic concerns to reviewers:

1. Considering my space limitations, I ask that reviews be no longer than three double-spaced pages. (The exceptions to this are so numerous as to render it almost a platitude, but it's a starting point.)

2. Avoid an "academic," jargon-heavy approach; if there seems to be no other way of handling the book, there's a good chance we shouldn't be reviewing it for mainstream, general interest book pages; the "tone" of most reviews should be considered but not stuffy, informed but not pedantic, lively but not "cute."

3. Unless it is the work of a highly celebrated author, a book that is more a failure than a success should be dealt with as efficiently (briefly) as possible; space is too precious; if it is a disappointing work from a major writer, people may be interested in the details of what went wrong.

4. Probably a stylistic quirk of mine more than anything else, but avoid a first-person approach ("I thought," "I once had an uncle who"); once again, exceptions are rife. (Most book editors will agree that their readers are more interested in the subject of the review than the reviewer himself.)

5. It's a critical cliche, but try to judge the book on its own terms—what it is trying to do and to what extent the book has achieved that goal; of course, you may also want to question the wisdom of what the book set out to do.

6. It's not necessary to make obvious commercial judgments for people ("Rush out and buy this!" "Don't waste your money"). The content of your review should allow people to make such decisions on their own.

7. An obvious point, but worth making: A review does more than just summarize the content of a book; it should include summary but as important—and usually more so—is a reviewer's response, putting the work into some sort of intellectual, cultural or aesthetic perspective. If all the book pages wanted to provide were summaries, we'd just run the publishers' press releases. Don't be afraid to digress to make a point, if the point is worth making.

8. If all you have to say is that a book's plot is too messy, the characters are under-developed, the theme is hackneyed, or the material is poorly organized, don't bother. Such freshman English word-spinning has become virtually meaningless.

9. If you don't understand some aspect of a book, say so; let the reader decide if it's your shortcoming or the book's.

10. If you don't think the book is worth reviewing (or you feel unqualified, or severely uninterested), speak up. Nobody gains from a formulaic review written with no enthusiasm; nevertheless, there may be occasions when you are specifically requested to review something of questionable merit because it has to be done for reasons known only to the book editor. Trust him.

In the review, identification must include author, title, and publisher. Interestingly, sales people at book stores are used to customers coming in and asking for books by general description—"that new gardening book they're all talking about," "the book written by the daughter of that movie star"—and can usually handle the request. Customers may have heard the author interviewed on radio or television, and their curiosity has been aroused. Even though veteran book store employees will know what to look for it is never in the best interest of the review to leave out, or abbreviate, the title.

Either in a block of smaller print above the actual review, or in the text of the review itself, the title, author, and publisher must appear. Many editors will also want the review to include length, price, if there are illustrations, if there is an introduction, or if the book is part of a series.

CHANGING DEFINITIONS

It's Not Always What it Seems

Next comes a rather difficult category, still a part of identification: What exactly is it that is being reviewed? Many newspaper readers use the terms *novel* and *book* interchangeably, and will not appreciate that a novel is primarily a work of fiction. A book is a book. All novels are books. All books are not novels. The determining aspect is whether the book is the result of a creative imagination (fiction), or based on fact (nonfiction).

Truman Capote.   Recent trends in publishing have made this test difficult. Truman Capote, who established an early reputation as a talented mid-century fiction writer, produced his classic *In Cold Blood* and announced that he had invented a new form of writing, a new art form, and he called it the nonfiction novel. (Journalists tend to forgive Capote almost anything, because one of his pronouncements was that he considered journalism the highest form of literature.)

In this book, Capote tells of the four members of a Kansas family who were killed by two men, who in turn were pursued, captured, and executed for their crime. It was primarily a job of reporting, except that Capote, who never met the members of the family, quoted them at length, and in addition described in great detail how they acted and how they felt. He also described in great detail the actions of the killers as they fled from lawmen. He did talk to them, but the degree of detail he uses is far more than one would expect in a work of nonfiction.

When challenged about this kind of writing, particularly in regard to the slain family, Capote said he had studied the habits, actions, and activities of that family more than anyone else, had lived in their house and had spent years in their home town. He said he was better equipped than anyone else to speak for them. Of course he did not personally hear them say what he quoted them as saying, but he insists that he knew them so well from his research that he knew just what they would have said in certain circumstances. No one ever accused author Capote of a lack of confidence.

Then Came Real Figures in Fiction

Later E. L. Doctorow used real figures in a slightly distorted historical novel called "Ragtime." Earlier fiction writers would routinely use real dates and locations, but only to support fictional characters. There are popular authors, such as Ray Bradbury and Kurt Vonnegut, who invent everything—new worlds, new machines, impossible situations.

Tom Wolfe.   Then there is the gifted Tom Wolfe, whose research is so thorough in works such as *The Right Stuff,* and whose style is so imaginative, that his book bears a strong resemblance to Capote's *In Cold Blood.*

The result is that it becomes increasingly difficult to categorize books. There is no problem with the obvious, but in these new, borderline cases, the best approach is to describe the book as to what it seems to be.

If it is confusing, let him say so. There is nothing wrong with suggesting that a certain work is extremely short for a novel, or lacks the character development one expects in a novel. The most important thing is to give the reader enough information to appreciate the review itself.

Summary is relatively easy to deal with in terms of what it is not. It is not synopsis. Falling into a chronological pattern in summarizing is the surest way to end up with a synopsis. It is also true that if the reviewer intentionally avoids a chronological account, he will probably end up writing a summary.

Opinion is the interesting facet of the literature review. Because there are thousands and thousands of words, there is more to comment on than in any other art. A book gives far more detail than a play or film or television program, and the reader can go back and re-read parts of the book, all the while enjoying it at his or her own pace, on his or her own time.

Perhaps this is why in literature there is a much better chance that the review will be mixed than in the other arts. There will be negative aspects of a positive review, and positive aspects of a negative review. Many books are popular, or sell well, although most readers could find something to object to. It might be a matter of too much sex and violence, too many foreign terms, too much background material, or it might be a matter of characters of some importance in the story who are not part of the story's resolution.

It is not that difficult to be critical in literature, but sensible reviewers as well as readers realize that a shortcoming or two does not mean the book is a failure.

No Doubt About the Language

One reason that negative aspects seem common in book reviews, regardless of the overall evaluation, is that the reviewer has before him exact language, and can easily support his opinion with examples. It is far more difficult to recall a line of bad dialogue in a play, or to remember precisely where a pianist missed a note in a concerto. Opinion in the literature review, because it is not a problem finding examples, is relatively easy to detail and support by example.

Many literature reviews can be charted as positive (or negative) at the beginning, having some mention of the negative (or positive) in the middle, then a reaffirmation of the positive (or negative) judgment at the end. The writer should leave enough time to thoroughly re-read his review to assure himself that the overall tone of the review is what he intended. This aspect of book reviews adds to the importance of beginning with a strong statement that is reflected at the end.

Writing in the *Houston Post*, Edward Osowski, a librarian who specializes in contemporary fiction, puts a new title in perspective, and here does a particularly effective job with summary. As is the case with most successful novels this book has a very involved plot and a strong underlying theme. Handling both in a relatively short review is a challenge.[1]

---

[1]Copyright © Edward J. Osowski.

WHAT HAPPENS WHEN 'WHAT IF' IS ALL TOO TRUE

Year Of The Gun, by Michael Mewshaw. 273 pp. Atheneum
By Edward J. Osowski

In the novels of Ken Follett, Jack Higgins and Frederick Forsyth—writers whose works Michael Mewshaw calls "faction docudramas"—fact and fiction blend in convoluted plots. Real people bump into fictional characters who play major roles in imaginary events based on the question, "What if?" What if Adolph Hitler had escaped to Venezuela? What if the Nazis had invaded Long Island? Such works fill a need to frighten the reader safely, to make him experience how badly things could have turned out, but fortunately did not.

Mewshaw prefaces Year of the Gun, his sixth novel, with a quote from Hemingway: "You cannot invent anything that could not actually happen. That is what we are supposed to do when we are at our best—make it all up—but make it up so truly that later it will happen that way." David Rayborne, the hero of Year of the Gun, carries the notion of "what if" one step further.

Using press releases, newspaper accounts, position papers and his own theories, Rayborne has prepared an outline for a book about the Italian terrorist organization the Red Brigade. Claiming to have conducted interviews with members of the organization, he secures a book contract from a publisher.

But the "what if" on which his book rests sets loose a chain of violent reactions—betrayals, attacks and murders. Rayborne's fatal mistake is that he has invented his fiction too well.

When the Red Brigade learns that the manuscript describes plans to kidnap former Premier Aldo Moro—an act they were planning—and that the kidnapping was to be directed by a woman with a German-sounding name—again, a fact that tallied with their secret plans—the possibility becomes too great to the leaders of the Red Brigade that Rayborne may have actually infiltrated a "cell" and secured the cooperation of members in preparing his book.

Rayborne's efforts to dupe the American public with his "fake" book is a cynical response to the newspaper cliches that have summarized the kidnappings, bombings and killings which seem to be such a part of Italian life. To the press, it is truly the "Year of the Gun." To Rayborne, living as an illegal alien, it is the "Year of the Sun" or the "Year of the Fun." There are more murders in Houston or Detroit, he points out to his boss, who won't listen to his objections. In Rayborne's mind, Americans are illiterate, incapable of understanding a discussion of the vagaries of Italian politics, and are concerned with violence and crime as they represent the collapse of civilization in Italy. Rayborne reminds a friend, "Americans don't have politics. We have VISA and Diner's Club."

How the Red Brigade learns of Rayborne's manuscript involves Alison Lopez, a successful photojournalist from Odessa and Nuevo Laredo, and Italo Bianchi, a professor of sociology in Rome and a member of the terrorist group. From Vietnam to Beirut, Lopez has followed the world's catastrophes, taming them through her lens.

In visiting Italy she hopes to prepare a book on the Red Brigade. When she learns of Rayborne's manuscript, she refuses to see it as fiction. She runs to Bianchi and hopes that by telling him of the book he will somehow arrange for her to meet members of the Red Brigade. No one knows, of course, that Bianchi is one of the terrorists. Although he counts Rayborne among his friends, Bianchi informs on him, ultimately sealing his own and Alison's fates.

Year of the Gun accomplishes the impossible. It injects life into the tired, formulaic patterns of the story of terrorist activity by telling it from the unique angle of two naive observers who accidentally become participants—Alison, who flirts with terrorism, but maintains a faith in her camera to keep her apart from the action she witnesses, and David, who fails to see the power of the words he sets to paper.

Mewshaw has not tried to beat Le Carre and all others at what they do so well. And he has not written an allegory in which his characters stumble around Rome looking for beauty, truth and knowledge. Mewshaw (whose two non-fiction works have been honored by the Texas Institute of Letters, including last year's tennis expose, Short Circuit) describes a Rome off the beaten tourist paths. It is gritty, dirty, real. Junkies deal dope and shoot up on the sidewalks. And the walls of buildings are covered with slogans like, "The machine gun is beautiful." As Rayborne admits early, it is behind this backdrop that life goes on, indifferent to those who try to draw lessons from it. Mewshaw's characters hold our attention as their mistakes and fumblings turn nightmares into reality.

There are other things that may be in the review, either under the heading of identification or simply other information of modest interest. The number of chapters is sometimes reported, as is the binding—hardback or paperback. The assumption seems to be that if no mention is made it is hardbound. If the book is oversize—larger than the average book—that will probably be in the review. Some books, in the general category of what are termed *art books*, will be oversize, but the basic novel will not. An appendix, bibliography, or footnotes may also be included.

The book may be one of a popular series of titles with similar themes, such as the late Ian Fleming and his famous secret agent James Bond, or a Travis McGee thriller, or a new Dick Francis race track mystery. The fact that a book is a new entry in a series or similar to earlier efforts should be in the review. Readers of book reviews should know if they are reading about a new, relatively unknown author, or an old favorite come to visit again. Simply mentioning the author's name may not be enough.

The number of characters and the location of the action are usually worked into the review. The time frame—current, last century, recent past—and the time span the book covers—2 days, 1 month, a century—are normally included. If the locale changes or if there are different locations, that can be mentioned.

How About the Ending?

In films and theater the reviewer often seems to be under some kind of unwritten oath not to spoil the event for the future viewer. This brought strong challenges to film writers commenting on "Rocky II" and "Rocky III," after the initial success of "Rocky." Most left little doubt about the outcome in the sequels, without actually giving away the endings. The excuse was that it was the acting and the fight scenes that made the movies enjoyable as much as their predictable outcomes.

Of course, with a murder mystery the reviewer who says "The butler did it" is in for a lot of trouble. In literature there is a similar situation. The reviewer must ask himself candidly if hinting at the outcome will spoil a future reader's experience. A literature review cannot be full of vague promises and veiled subjects; there is no reason not to provide concrete examples to support opinion. Ideally, the reviewer tells a great deal about the book and its author, including, perhaps, how it all ends, yet leaves much for the eventual reader to find out for him or herself.

Yet there is good reason to at least consider summarizing a plot, including the ending. There is a secondary audience for book reviews, as well as reviews of the other arts, consisting of readers who do not plan to read the book, or to see the play, but want to know about it. In other words, many newspaper readers enjoy reading about plays and concerts, art exhibits and new books, but have no interest in seeing or reading them. But they feel that, if something is of interest to their neighbors, they themselves want to at least be aware of it. The book review too short on summary leaves them unhappy.

THERE IS AN INTELLIGENT AUDIENCE

As a rule, the reader of the book review is going to be more intellectual, certainly better read, and probably more critical of the reviewer than the reader of a film or popular music review. The audience, both for literature and the literature review, is comparatively small. A runaway best seller might sell 200,000 copies in hardback and perhaps 4 or 5 million softbound.

Even with two readers to a copy that is still fewer consumers than a third-rate prime-time television show will attract in one evening. The literature review is aimed at an elite audience, and must be treated accordingly. It is a highly sophisticated and difficult kind of writing, and the writer must travel with care and spend as much time thinking as writing.

In literary criticism, perhaps more so than the other arts, it is occasionally necessary to consult experts. In a modern thriller with a space science background it could be important to determine if the accounts of space activity and technology are realistic. The reviewer may not be able to determine if what is written is realistic and accurate, and may need to ask the newspaper's science writer for help. If the newspaper staff is too small to include an expert in the field, the reviewer should look outside. Just as authors consult physicians and attorneys to assure the authenticity of their tales, so should reviewers look for expertise to keep track of the authors.

This is not only legitimate, but necessary. Nothing makes a reviewer and his newspaper look worse than to overlook an obvious technical flaw in a book being reviewed.

Literature is the creation of a mind, not muscles, not physical talent or dexterity. It is a mental effort of the highest order, and literary criticism should be no less.

Chapter Thirteen
The Ethics of the Business

NEWSPAPER LAW AND LIBEL

For about 2 centuries, American journalists have rejoiced in the fact that theirs is a profession with its own constitutional guarantee. Jurists have agreed that the First Amendment means that there shall be no prior restraint of the press, but this does not give carte blanche, because the companion interpretation is that after the news story or editorial or review appears, the newspaper is responsible for its contents.

After years of abuse of and by the press, a body of law has emerged that goes by the vague and unofficial term of *Newspaper Law.* A collection of judicial decisions at various levels, the most significant ones coming from the United States Supreme Court, it consists primarily of precendential ways of dealing with matters of libel and invasion of privacy. These are common law matters, based on court decisions, and constantly subject to change, as compared to statutory laws, which are acts passed by a legislative body that can only be changed or revoked by that same council or legislature or congress.

Libel is a published defamation of an identifiable person or persons. In recent years the courts have held that broadcast constitutes publication, so a broadcast defamation is usually considered libelous, rather than slanderous (*slander* is the term reserved for oral defamation). This is because libel is considered the greater offense, and because some broadcasts reach many times the audience a newspaper could claim, it stands to reason that the more serious charge of libel is appropriate.

Identification need not be by name; the courts have held that if an interested reader can figure out who the subject of a report is, then identification is present. Just because the reviewer does not mention the leading actor in a play by name does not mean the actor has not been identified.

Just What Is Defamation?

Defamation is the tricky aspect of libel, and, in large part, depends on contemporary mores. During the 1950s, an unwed couple living together was unacceptable to the general public. If a news story identified Mary Jones and Sam Smith as living at the same address, and modest effort revealed it to be a single-family home, the statement could be held to be defamatory because the implication was that the two were cohabiting without being married.

A quarter of a century later the situation had changed dramatically, and young and old couples live together without being married, married women retain their maiden names for professional reasons, and what had been actionable is now acceptable. That is how common law works.

Three traditional defenses against a libel action have developed over the years. *Provable Truth*, where the truth of the statement can be proven in court, is considered an absolute defense. This is the defense that allows reporters to report, without fear of retribution by the subject of their reports, as long as they are accurate. This defense is seldom called upon because its very existence means that a libel action would be unsuccessful.

In similar fashion, the defense of *Privilege*, which means that a newspaper (or radio or television station) cannot be held liable for defamatory statements as long as it is producing an accurate report of a legislative or legal proceding, is seldom applied. The fact that this defense exists and has been recognized by the courts is enough.

The third defense is the difficult one, and the one most invoked by reviewers and critics. It is called *Fair Comment*, and means that as long as a reviewer or critic is giving an evaluation of a public person's performance, the report is not actionable even though it is defamatory. It is usually reserved for comment on activity in the arts, but can also include those in the worlds of sports and politics.

Even the President of the United States must accept this right of the press, as in the 1950s when Harry Truman's daughter Margaret was pursuing a professional singing career. Paul Hume of the *Washington Post* wrote "She is flat a good deal of the time. . . . She cannot sing with anything approaching professional finish. . . . She communicates almost nothing of the music she presents."[1] Daddy Harry was furious, and dashed off a blistering note to the newspaper, which cheerfully published it. There was no doubt that this time the press came out ahead of the Pres.

Those in the Public Eye Are Targets

This Fair Comment aspect of libel, the most likely to change from decade to decade, if not year to year, is why publications of all sizes and stripes must have con-

---

[1]Truman, M. (1973). *Harry S. Truman*. New York: William Morrow.

stant access to legal advice, and why those writing about libel must constantly issue the caveat that things can, and do, change.

People who willingly place themselves in the limelight for profit must take their lumps from the press. This is what is known as fair comment, and applies to those who have become, in the eyes of our courts, public figures. Of course what constitutes a public figure is something else to be argued and decided, based on the times and the community. Law reviews are full of interesting decisions on libel actions, and two early important decisions are typical of the many that have been issued in support of a newspaper's right to comment. The first is a case journalists love to talk about.

In the late 19th century a musical group of questionable talent was making its way around the midwest. As they performed in a small Iowa town, the Cherry Sisters incurred the wrath of a local critic. His words in turn were picked up by the *Des Moines Leader*, which gave this account of the event:

> Billy Hamilton, of the Odebolt Chronicle, gives the Cherry Sisters the following graphic write-up on their late appearance in his town:
>
> "Effie is an old jade of 50 summers, Jessie a frisky filly of 40, and Addie, the flower of the family, a capering monstrosity of 35. Their long skinny arms, equipped with talons at the extremeties, swung mechanically and anon waved frantically at the suffering audience. The mouths of their rancid features opened like caverns, and sounds like the wailing of damned souls issued therefrom. They pranced around the stage with a motion that suggested a cross between the danse du ventre and a fox trot—strange creatures with painted faces and hideous mien. Effie is spavined, Addie is stringhalt, and Jessie, the only one who showed her stockings, has legs and calves as classic in their outlines as the curves of a broom handle."

The outraged sisters sued—not the Odebolt paper, with its limited resources, but the larger, more affluent *Leader*. Even then litigants knew that when it comes time for judicial redress you look for "deep pockets," even though that paper's sin was merely repeating, rather than originating, the offensive remarks. It made no difference; the sisters lost, the newspaper won [Cherry v. Des Moines Leader, 114 Ia. 298 (1901)], and ever since those in the business of offering fair comment have offered an occasional toast to Billy and the Cherry Sisters.

Not Just Entertainers Are Involved

A case in 1930 broadened the subject. A high school football coach was severely criticized in the sports pages, and he sued. He lost, the court ruling "Ball players and athletes, like public officials, actors, authors, musicians, and artists are objects of interest to the public. The publication is not libelous unless actuated by malice" [Hoeppner v. Dunkirk Printing Co., 254 N.Y. 95 (1930)].

But just as these cases support an important aspect of criticism, they also draw a vital line between the public and the private lives of public figures. Briefly, the distinction is this: When the public figure has made an attempt to keep his private life to him or herself, and the press pries into it, the defense of fair comment will not apply. But when the individual has made no attempt to keep anything to him or herself, it does.

When the wonderful dancer Fred Astaire died in 1987, and tributes and recollections poured forth, it was remarkable how little the nation knew about the private man. He had done his best to keep his personal life to himself, and the press, for the most part, concerned itself with his acting, singing, and dancing.

During the course of his career there were many who were savage in their denouncement of his singing and acting. That was fair comment, in the truest sense, and the great dancer never objected. But there was little prying into his private life.

Consider next the young film star who freely discusses with the press who she or he is living with; or the actor or actress who speaks freely of ingestants he or she has tried; or the aging star who writes a "tell-it-all" book revealing in sensational detail the intimate experiences he or she has shared with half of Hollywood. These people have little to say when the press comes snooping around, anxious to sell stories to gossip-hungry readers.

The Lady Got Mad: The Burnett Case

But things were different when actress Carol Burnett took on the *National Enquirer*, a weekly publication sold primarily in supermarkets that specilizes in gossip and inuendo [Burnett v. National Enquirer, 144 Cal. App. 3d 991, (1983)]. It had printed a story about Burnett's behavior in a restaurant, an account that was clearly defamatory.

When she threatened suit, the paper claimed fair comment, but her reply was that this was a private part, not a public aspect, or her existence. It was a grueling and costly battle, but she won. Unfortunately, the cost of the victory was considerable. Once the libel action started it became a matter of public record, and could be repeated by any publication that wished to use the defamatory material. Privilege protected other publications that might have hesitated to use the story initially, but now could run it with impunity. This is what Burnett's friends were referring to when they urged her not to sue, saying it would cost more than it would be worth. But the lady was mad, and determined that the newspaper would not go unchallenged, at least in this instance. Certainly there was some satisfaction in her triumph.

However, editors at all levels would rather avoid such litigation. Both critic and reviewer will normally confine their remarks to the part of the public figure's life that is unquestionably public. Responsible newspapers will not sacrifice sensitivity for sensation.

Invasion of Privacy

Invasion of privacy is the other aspect of newspaper law that can cause problems for reviewers and critics, although here gossip columnists have more to worry about. Briefly, defenses against libel are applied to protect the press, although libel itself is a charge against the press; and invasion of privacy practices are designed to protect the individual from the press.

Simply put, protection against invasion of privacy guarantees the private citizen's right to be left alone. Those who believe their privacy has been invaded need not prove or even charge defamation; it is enough to show that the media were indeed invasive. In general terms, the press can deal with public figures in public places without fear of suit; but when the venue is private, there may be problems.

As a rule, the writing of both critic and reviewer goes through a copy desk (although there are times when deadline pressure is such that the writer edits his or her own copy, and even adds a headline), and copy editors are trained to be attuned to the dangers of libel and invasion of privacy. Still, an amusements or arts editor can hardly be happy with a writer who continually invites litigation. Win or lose, it is an expensive process.

CONFLICTS OF INTEREST: LEGAL, YES. BUT ETHICAL?

Although the First Amendment to the Constitution offers the journalist freedom not enjoyed by his counterparts in other parts of the world, it also holds the door open for what could at best be described as *unethical behavior*. Clearly the newspaper writer can have an effect on the fortunes of those he writes about, particularly in the entertainment business. What's to keep the reporter from soliciting a few bucks for a favorable review? Mainly his conscience and his editor, and this is certainly not an area of widespread abuse, although the potential is there.

This difficult area of ethical considerations starts off with the free pass, which seems to be of no real concern to anyone, even though it could be considered a conflict of interest. The reviewer, or the baseball writer, manages to be objective even though the subject of his report is paying his way, and even giving him a couple of hot dogs as well.

The Junket

But the matter reaches a critical level in an activity called the *junket*. This is when a reporter goes somewhere for a period of time to gather information for his newspaper, and someone else pays the bills. The conflicts of interest are obvious, because the bills can easily be in the several thousand dollar range.

The Caribbean Cruise

Here is how it may begin. A large travel agency calls. It is putting together a new Caribbean Cruise plan, and is inviting members of the press along for the maiden voyage. The trip will last 2 weeks, and includes stops at six islands. The cost to the general public could be well over $4,000. All the newspaper has to do is send along a reporter–photographer, and it will get great copy and pictures in return.

These stories are popular, the editor knows, and are seen as good circulation builders. What's more, other area newspapers are sending reporters, and he does not want to be left out. Even though he knows that the stories that will result from this cruise will invariably be favorable, and he is leery of the conflict of interest aspect, he does not have a spare $4,000.

Some cynics have spoken of offering a handsome prize for the first unfavorable travel story to come from such an expenses-paid trip, confident that it will never be claimed.

An Invitation to Summer Camp

Across the hall in the newspaper building the sports editor picks up the telephone. The caller is the sports information director of a professional football team, who announces that they are putting together a media trip to the team's training camp, and invites the newspaper to send a sports reporter along. The team will provide transportation, food and lodging, and a photographer.

The sports editor knows that interest in the team is building, because it drafted a local player recently. Not only that, the television stations have already accepted the offer. Finally, even though there are funds to pay the reporter's way, there are no motels or restaurants nearby, and even if there were the writer would miss out on mealtime and dormitory activity.

It is either accept the team's offer, or miss out on good sports copy and alienate your readers. This is an ongoing problem with no easy solution. Of course the newspaper accepts the team's generosity, and tries to remain objective in spite of it.

A Trip to the West Coast

Now the entertainment desk has its own problem. A major television network is arranging a tour for television writers, who will be flown to the network's west coast studios, there to see advance episodes of next season's programs, to interview past and future stars, and to talk to directors and producers about the state of the art. And to get a trip to Disneyland.

The cost to the newspaper would be prohibitive, even if it were the kind of thing the newspaper could buy. To the network it is little or nothing, and everybody is going. To be fair, this type of junket has not been charged with abuse, as many television writers have been as savage during their visits to the production studios as when they stay at home and watch on their own sets. But again someone with something to gain is shelling out big bucks, and the newspapers are accepting.

Problems of the Junket

One thing that makes the existence of the junket a potential problem is that newspapers are not always the most beneficent of employers, and often fringe benefits, such as an occasional junket, keep good writers from leaving for greener pastures. But financial considerations aside, the greater problem is that these junkets produce good, readable copy, stories, and pictures that often are simply not available elsewhere.

The potential of conflict of interest is weighed against service to subscribers. There are, of course, no strings attached to any of these offers, and reporters are encouraged to be as objective as they are able. The junket, as it presents a conflict of interest, is a journalistic fact of life. In the perfect world, the newspaper will pay for everything. In an imperfect one, you do the best you can. But an awareness of the dangers is the first step in preventing the abuse.

THE POWER OF THE PEN: WISE GUY WRITING

Another ethical consideration facing the entertainment writer has to do with amateurs, and includes what many call *wise guy* writing. The critical comment can be a powerful and savage weapon if misused. This misuse may occur because colleagues on the newspaper, as well as readers, react more to the negative comment than to the positive one. Every reviewer has heard "I love it when you blast someone." The writer replies that he only gave them what they deserved, but can hardly escape noticing that his positive reviews pass with no comment.

In the case of professionals, critical standards should be exacting. After all, this is their business, they are making money, and they are fully aware of the show business axiom that bad publicity is better than no publicity. But amateurs, putting in time and effort for the love of the art, deserve kinder treatment. In this instance, the reviewer will realize it is possible to offer positive criticism, and that any review can be a mixture of the positive and negative.

But avoid the cheap shots and the wise guy remarks. They are not needed, and cheapen the writer personally. Although he may become known for his vocabulary, or sharp pen or tongue, he may lose his reputation for critical ability and perception.

ENTERTAINMENT WRITERS CAN BE WATCHDOGS

Journalists like to refer to the *watchdog* function of the newspaper, as it keeps an eye on those who make our laws and spend our money. In the entertainment arena, the newspaper serves as a watchdog in two ways. It keeps a close eye on those who take money for their efforts, and an even closer eye on what comes to town.

In the first case, when a famous person arrives, his local sponsor may suggest that there is a particularly conscientious writer who will be covering his performance, and that this writer is earning a reputation for high standards. "In that case I'd better get some rest," the star says. "This play's bad enough without me lousing it up more." And even though the vehicle may be lacking, the actor works hard and the audience is generally satisfied.

But the local host could also report to the star that there is no one with any taste for miles around. The local paper will send someone to cover the play, but they never know what they are doing. The actor, tired from weeks on the road and looking forward only to the end of the tour, walks listlessly through his role, content to merely chalk up one more stop on this ill-advised trip. When the reviewer is not paying attention, it is the public that suffers.

The other area of watchdogging is when a writer, or an entire amusements staff, has high standards and objects so violently to shoddy material and performances that those who deal in such areas keep away from that city. Consider the touring show featuring an actress who spends most of her time taking off her clothes, appearing in a play that is little more than an excuse for nudity and vulgarity.

An audience exists for such efforts, otherwise they would never get on the road, but they are not welcome everywhere. The producer who packages such shows will assemble a group of actors and actresses, put a cute name on the package, and begin rehearsing the bumps, grinds, and gags. Meanwhile he sends out brochures and announcements to cities and towns across the country, hoping to book shows in theaters close enough together to guarantee an audience every night. This is how he makes his money.

In due time the local impresario gets the word, and wonders if he should book the show. The arrangements might be that he must guarantee 500 seats, and that he gets 50% of all sales above that, plus a share of the concessions. It is his business to know if his community will turn out in enough numbers to make money.

Perhaps last year he brought in a similar show, and sold out his 1000-seat hall. So he says "Sure, I'll sign up," and the tasteless show comes to town. But supposing that, when he brought in a like attraction last year, the local press took him to task, roundly criticized him for the production, and in general gave him a bad public image.

Suppose further that as a result of this negative press, future attractions, ones that normally do well, suffered at the gate. In this instance, given his experience of last year, he will probably turn down the new offering.

There are those who claim this puts too much power in the hands of the press, but that will not hold up. What if the locals really want to see the raunchy collection of gals and gags the promoter has put together? If that is the case it will come to town regardless of what the newspaper says. The promoter will find some place to stage his show, and the newspaper will not have denied its readers the freedom of choice to see what they want.

THE HUNTER BECOMES THE HUNTED

Still another consideration in this discussion applies to critic and reviewer alike. As they wax critical of artists and the arts, they also invite criticism. It is not unusual for those who make judgments to become themselves the object of attack. This should be the standard, not the exception, in the newspaper reviewing business. There is an old saying editors like to repeat: "The Democrats say we favor the Republicans, the Republicans say we favor the Democrats. We must be doing something right." It is a good lesson.

Although it is not really a normal part of the position, coming under attack should not be an unfamiliar experience for the critic or reviewer. This attack can come in any of four ways. First is the letter to the editor, complaining about unfair treatment, lack of sensitivity, or faulty judgment. The usual practice is to print the letter without comment, which demonstrates the newspaper's objectivity.

The second attack comes when an influential person telephones the editor to complain. This is a little more of a problem. The editor will consult the writer, and we assume will trust him, and will tell the caller that the newspaper stands behinds its reviewers. One can only hope that the editor will not say "Ease up. We can't afford to antagonize this guy." That is not good journalism.

Another type of attack comes in the form of word of mouth spread among those in the field by those offended. This can be unpleasant, but there's not much the writer can do but stick to his guns and remember the Republicans and the Democrats.

Finally, the reviewer or critic can be attacked in other media, drawing unfavorable criticism for his writing from those in television, other newspapers, or area magazines. But both know that in journalism the surest way to kill something is to ignore it, just as the best way to be sure that the attack continues is to respond to it. Even if they are saying bad things about us, at least they know we are here, and we are having some effect.

Epilogue

Now the reviewer is ready to go to work. He enters the theater, takes his seat on the end of the third row, and nods to the critic seated near him. She nods back, and each turns to the stage as the curtain goes up.

Just as the whisperer says "They're the critics," they have to wonder: Do they do their best work if they are known, or in relative obscurity? Obviously it is impossible to perform on television without becoming instantly recognizable, and it often seems as difficult to become recognized as a print journalist.

The reviewer should take advantage of this; he functions best when his presence is not obvious. The professional company will present essentially the same performance night after night, but the amateurs will not, and a phrase heard frequently behind the curtain just before it opens is that the reviewer is in the house.

He should try to remain unknown. He does this by arriving at the theater or concert hall just before the opening curtain, rather than making a noisy late entrance. At intermission he keeps to himself, working on his notes, starting to compose a lead. Even at a film the time immediately after the performance is too valuable to waste chit-chatting with others.

Over a period of time the reviewer, like the critic, will develop a local following as well as a local reputation. If he achieves the kind of stature where he is asked to address high school music and drama groups, so much the better. This is certainly in keeping with his, and the newspaper's, role as friend of the arts.

The difference is in whether he seeks such recognition actively, or accepts it as a reward for his efforts. Those who see the entertainment assignment as a route to personal glory and accomplishment are doomed to fail. Those who see it as a way to make a real contribution to the arts will succeed.

Selected Reading List

Any reading list that attempts to cover all the arts is by definition incomplete.

This is a beginning.

ARCHITECTURE

Contemporary Architects (2nd ed.). (1988). New York: St. James Press.

Kostoff, S. (1985). *A history of architecture: Settings and rituals.* New York: Oxford University Press.

Poppeliers, J., Chambers, S. A. & Schwartz, N. B. (1977). *What style is it.* Washington, DC: The Preservation Press of The National Trust for Historical Preservation.

ART AND SCULPTURE

Arnason, H. H. (1968). *History of modern art. Painting, sculpture, architecture.* Englewood Cliffs/New York: Prentice-Hall, Harry N. Abrams.

De la Croix, H., & Tansey, R. G. (1986). *Art through the ages.* New York: Harcourt Brace Jovanovich.

Gombrich, E. H. (1953). *The story of art.* London: Phaedon Press.

Hunter, S., & Jacobus, J. (1985). *Modern art. Painting, sculpture, architecture.* Englewood Cliffs/New York: Prentice-Hall, Harry N. Abrams.

Pelfrey, R., & Hall-Pelfrey, M. (1985). *Art and mass media.* New York: Harper & Row.

DANCE

Anderson, J. (1974). *A history of dance.* New York: Newsweek Books.

Clarke, M., & Crisp, C. (1981). *The history of dance.* New York: Crown Publishing.

Jowitt, D. (1977). *Dance beat.* New York: Dekker.

Kraus, R., & Chapman, S. (1981). *History of the dance in art and education* (2nd ed.). Englewood Cliffs/New York: Prentice-Hall.

Murray, L. (1980). *Inside dance.* New York: St. Mary's Press.

DRAMA

Brook, P. (1968). *The empty space.* New York: Atheneum.

Clurman, H. (1972). *On directing.* New York: Macmillan.

Grotowski, J. (1969). *Towards a poor theatre*. London: Methven.

Kott, J. (1964). *Shakespeare, our contemporary*. Garden City, NY: Doubleday.

Saint Denis, M. (1960). *Theatre, the rediscovery of style*. New York: Theatre Arts Books.

Stanislavsky, C. (1946). *An actor prepares*. New York: Theatre Arts Books.

Stanislavsky, C. (1948). *My life in art*. New York: Theatre Arts Books.

FILM

Kawin, B. F. (1987). *How movies work*. New York: Macmillan.

Mast, G. (1986). *A short history of the movies* (4th ed.). New York: Macmillan.

Kawin, B., & Cohen, M. (Eds.). (1985). *Film theory and criticism: Introductory readings* (3rd ed.). New York and Oxford: Oxford University Press.

LITERATURE

Adams, J. D. (1965). *Speaking of books—and life*. New York: Holt, Rinehart and Winston.

Hart, J. D. (Ed.). (1983). *The Oxford companion to American literature* (5th ed.). New York: Oxford University Press.

The Norton Reader (6th ed.). (1984). New York: W. W. Norton.

Rees, R. A., & Menikoff, B. (Eds.). (1969). *The short story—An introductory anthology*. Boston: Little Brown.

Wolfe, T., & Johnson, E. W. (Eds.). (1973). *The new journalism*. New York: Harper & Row.

MUSIC

Baker, T. (1984). *Baker's biographical dictionary of musicians*. New York: G. Schirmer.

Grout, D. J. (1980). *A history of western music*. New York: W. W. Norton.

Harder, P. (1980). *Harmonic materials in tonal music: A programmed course*. Boston: Allyn & Bacon.

Kerman, J. (1980). *Listen*. New York: Worth Publishers.

Machlis, J. (1984). *The enjoyment of music*. New York: W. W. Norton.

Randel, D. (Ed.). (1986). *The new Harvard dictionary of music*. Cambridge, MA: The Belknap Press of Harvard University Press.

Spaeth, S. (1963). *The importance of music*. New York: Fleet Publishing.

TELEVISION

Millerson, G. (1985). *The technique of television production* (11th ed.). London and Boston: Focal Press.

Sterling, C. H., & Kittross, J. M. (1978). *Stay tuned: A concise history of American broadcasting*. Belmont, CA: Wadsworth.

Zettl, H. (1973). *Sight-sound-motion. Applied media aesthetics*. Belmont, CA: Wadsworth.

Zettl, H. (1984). *Television production handbook* (4th ed.). Belmont, CA: Wadsworth.

Index